Aloha, Welcome To

SAM CHOY'S KITCHEN

Other books by Chef Sam Choy

Sam Choy's Cuisine Hawaii
Pleasant Hawaii, Inc.

With Sam Choy: Cooking From the Heart
Mutual Publishing

Sam Choy's Cooking: Sam Choy's Island Cuisine
(The Choy of Cooking)
Mutual Publishing

The Choy of Seafood: Sam Choy's Pacific Harvest
Mutual Publishing

Sam Choy's Island Flavors
Hyperion

Sam Choy's Poke: Hawai'i's Soul Food
Mutual Publishing

Aloha, Welcome To

SAM CHOY'S KITCHEN

*Cooking Doesn't Get Any Easier
Than This!*

Aloha, Welcome To

SAM CHOY'S KITCHEN

*Cooking Doesn't Get Any Easier
Than This!*

By Chef Sam Choy
and Lynn Cook

Recipes Edited by
Joannie Dobbs, Ph.D, C.N.S.

*Featuring recipes from Sam's television show,
Sam Choy's Kitchen, as well as some traditional favorites*

Mutual Publishing

Library of Congress Catalog Card
Number: 99-66957

First Printing, November 1999

Second Printing, April 2000

2 3 4 5 6 7 8 9

Design by Gonzalez Design Company

Layout by Mardee Domingo & Jane Hopkins

Photographs by Ray Wong on pages: i, iii, iv, ix, xi, xii, xvi, xvii, xix, 146

All remaining photographs by Douglas Peebles

Quilt Pattern Kaulana Ka Lehua O Hawai'i
used with permission from quiltmaker Annette Sumada; Eleanor Ahuna designer

ISBN 1-56647-282-2

Mutual Publishing
1215 Center Street, Suite 210
Honolulu, Hawaii 96816
Ph: (808) 732-1709
Fax: (808) 734-4094
e-mail: mutual@lava.net
www.mutualpublishing.com

Printed in Taiwan

Dedication

Today her favorites are poi, bread, rice, and cinnamon crackers.
Tomorrow, who knows. But, I'll tell you what,
this granddaughter of ours just loves food.

Samantha Pua Mohala Choy

Our Angel — Tini

I dedicate this book to Samantha and all the young ones, lucky to be
growing up in Hawai'i in a time when we are again celebrating food.
We are bringing back the rich, simple taste of mom and dad's kitchen.

My hope is that parents everywhere encourage their young ones
to read this book and watch Sam Choy's Kitchen. When the kids say,
"Wow, that looks 'ono—can we have that for dinner?" say,
"Yes, let's cook it together!" I guarantee it will taste even better
than if you ate it in my restaurant!

Pretty soon, Tini can cook with me. I can hardly wait!

Table of Contents

Never Trust A Skinny Chef

We'll Be Right Back

Stay Tuned

Thank You For Joining Us

See You Next Time

Introduction
Welcome to Sam Choy's Kitchen

Aloha, and welcome to Sam Choy's Kitchen. Boy, I'll tell you what. We're going to have some fun. This book is just the printed version of my TV show. Both are filled with easy cooking. I take you, step-by-step, to a finished culinary delight that you can proudly serve your family and friends. Even if you think you can only make "holy water" (that's when you fill a pot with water, put it on the stove on high and boil the heck out of it) this book can make you a cook.

It doesn't get any easier than this!

The recipes don't have dozens of ingredients. Each one has just a few minutes of prep-time, a few minutes of actual cooking and lots of good eating. What you need to do is get a "vocabulary" of eight to ten main dishes. Get comfortable with them. Follow my recipe but don't be afraid to add some ingredients of your own. You may love garlic and onion and cilantro as much as I do. Or, you may think cilantro tastes like an old sofa. Substitute fresh basil. Cut down on the garlic or the hot peppers. Add more onions or soy sauce. Make the taste work for you.

Many of my dishes are light on the oil, stir-fried seafood with vegetables. Sometimes I just have to add the butter. And, our motto then is, "more butter—mo' better." Not every meal, just sometimes when nothing else will do.

All you need to start down the road to gourmet cooking, Sam Choy-style, is a couple of sharp knives, a wok, a steamer and a good deep kettle. You also need to forget all the tales you have heard about "how hard it is to cook fish" or "how easy it is to ruin a prime rib." Believe that you can do this. Eating good food is one of the great joys in life. Cooking it and serving it and watching others enjoy your labors is an even greater joy. Getting the whole family involved is the biggest charge of all.

I was so lucky. My family made cooking an event. Everyone was included. My folks, Clariemoana and Hung Sam Choy, are my inspiration. They shared everything with me. And, they taught me to share with you. Now, the next step is for you to take the recipes I offer, make them, then make them better and share them with others. There should be no secrets. Share your success and enjoy the pleasure that sharing brings in return.

CREATING THE DISH

When you cook, think about the ingredients. Imagine the delicious creation you are about to make. Think of it in layers. The basic ingredient is the first layer. Always use the sweetest, freshest fish, chicken, pork, beef, or seafood you can find. Be sure you don't overcook. Remember, food continues to cook after you take it off the heat. Believe my instructions. When I say "three minutes on each side" that doesn't mean six. Cook it longer and it is often ruined! For the next layer use one of the many marinades or spice combinations to enhance your main ingredient. Top it all off with a sauce that adds flavor and helps the magic of the dish to happen. Now decorate the dish, make it beautiful with edible flowers scattered on top or little bow ties of green onion around the potatoes. The extra minute or two that the decorating takes can turn a dinner into a feast. Rice, pasta or stir-fried vegetables balance the main course. Remember, light-heavy-light. Balance the courses; light salad, heavier fish with sauce, light vegetable stir-fry or rice.

Dessert, of course, stands on its own. It doesn't really matter how full you are. When a luscious dessert is served, the fluffy mounds of chocolate and the mouth-watering juices glistening on Hawai'i's succulent fruits tempt the eyes and convince the stomach. It's the perfect way to end a perfect meal.

Now ! Let's Cook!!

Producing the Shows, Creating the Food

Dateline — HONOLULU, HAWAI'I — *"The toughest part of doing a television show with Sam Choy?" ponders show director and producer Laurie La Madrid. "Well, the really tough part is having to stay around after the filming is done to eat all that great food!"*

*S*miling, La Madrid echoes the sentiments of the entire crew and management of KHNL-TV when she says that doing anything with Sam Choy is a joy. "Sam is the most giving person I have ever worked with. He just wants to share his love of food, of cooking. He wants everyone to know how easy it is to create wonderful dishes. He wants to make it easy for his viewers to cook. My husband loves Sam because working on the show even inspired me to go home and whip up some of the easy dishes Sam presents!"

John Fink, president and general manager of KHNL-TV News 8 describes the beginning of Sam Choy's Kitchen as a, "hand-shake deal built entirely on trust. What was basically a 'what if' conversation between Sam and the station became a reality in January, 1996, with the first Sam Choy's Kitchen show." Fink says Sam seemed like the perfect ambassador for Hawai'i to present the cuisine of the Islands. He had the heart, his business was growing. And it seemed like the perfect match. "We started with minimal sponsorship. Everyone at the station was excited, the entire staff loved Sam from the first shoot. It was just too much fun not to succeed!"

SUCCESS ! !

Succeed it has. Nearing the 200 show mark, things are getting better every time. The show has gone on location as Sam has opened restaurants in Japan and Guam. The popularity of the show has generated re-runs. The show is running during prime time in Guam. Conversations are in the works for national distribution, and possibly even a show with a live audience.

La Madrid is producer number four. Michael Ainsworth was first, followed by Kevin Kau and Paul Eblen. Each producer, and the entire show crew, echo La Madrid's sentiments when she says, "I don't call this work. We are like a big family. We just have too much fun! With Sam, what you see is what you get—just a sincere guy looking into the camera, saying 'you can do this too.' Not that the shows are predictable. There's always what we call the 'Sam', or the 'flaming pans', and a wide variety of guests." From an internationally known chef, like Sam's good friend Emeril Lagasse, to an Upcountry Maui farmer growing Sam's favorite herbs, the guest list is always varied.

You might assume that the "hot spot" on Sam's show would be the guest slot. Not so. Ask the cameraman to Sam's right. He's one of the show's three cameramen who occupies the "hot spot." When Sam does one of his famous wok dishes, "burning off the wine" or "browning the shrimp," its the cameraman who gets toasted. Instead of "hazardous duty pay" they usually take extra servings of the day's delicious fare. How does the crew stay slim? By only shooting the shows a couple of times a month, then jogging a lot in between.

EIGHT-AND-A-HALF MINUTES

A 30-minute cooking show, explains the producer, actually has only eight-and-a-half minutes of cooking time. The remainder of the time is taken up by the welcome, description of the dishes to be prepared, a few stories from Sam, interviewing guests, or promoting one of the many community public service events and programs that Sam gives support to. Even though a theme or set of recipes is planned, everyone waits for the moment of "Sam." The producer says, "No matter what is planned, our chef always adds the 'Sam.' He is like a great painter, adding that artistic touch or whimsical moment that is pure entertainment."

HOW TO FIND YOUR 'INNER CIRCLE OF FLAVORS'

And, where do you put it once you've found it?

In the words of Chef Sam Choy:
First thing—open the refrigerator.
See what's inside. Then, go to the

cupboard shelves. What's there? What foods do you keep? What canned goods? Which spices? What kind of things are in your freezer? Jot down your inventory. Make this list, then spend some time thinking about what flavors you have found.

Most of the flavors and spices are there because you like them. O.K., not counting that "Food from Route 66" basket your auntie brought back from her Greyhound trip. What you have in your kitchen tells you what you are familiar with and what you like. That doesn't mean that you aren't willing to experiment, it just means you already know a bit about your taste buds.

Now, begin to compile a mental, or written, list of the meals you have loved. That includes everything from a gourmet meal, to plate lunch, to what your mom and aunties served on Sundays. That, my friends, is your inner circle of flavors. No magic formula, no high-tech testing involved. Just like when you watch me cook on TV. What you see is what you get and, hopefully, what you like to eat. So now you know. Get cooking !!

Think about this. A thousand pounds of fried poke. That's what we serve in our restaurants every week! That's what I call mainstream. All my restaurants have at least one fried poke on the menu. Fishing with my dad, I learned early in life which fishes were good for eating raw. When I started cooking I started playing around with flavors, seeing what could be done with the raw fish. So easy. You can do it at home. Serve a seared poke, some Drunken Shrimp and maybe a Seafood Salad. Boy, I'll tell you what, served with Sam's beer, you got a feast!

Pupu's are an art form. They allow you to be creative. They allow you to take chances. After all, this isn't the entrée, it is just the fun beginning. Guests on my show, from athletes to rock stars, have had lots of fun creating pupus and finger foods. Invite your family and guests into the kitchen while you create. Enjoy!

My annual Sam Choy Poke Contest is part of Aloha Festivals. Now folks who love to cook and love raw fish are inventing incredible new recipes to enter. That means we will have even more 'ono preparations to choose from.

Raw fish, sashimi, is served all over the world. Trendy sushi bars are everywhere. Not everyone likes raw fish, but you can bet that most folks have tried it at least once. Since I have been on the road with my cooking—as a guest chef in various parts of the mainland and as part of the Hawai'i Visitors and Convention Bureau's Chefs of Aloha—I am beginning to see poke, like a Poke Salad, up in one of Napa's trendy restaurants. It's like how we started to see seared 'ahi not long after it was a feature of most Hawai'i restaurants. I tell you, many hot food trends start in Hawai'i.

Pesto Brie Wheel

Serves 6 to 8

Excellent with veggies, toasted bread, or crackers,
this elegant round of mellow cheese takes on an island personality
with macadamia nuts and ginger cilantro pesto.

3 tablespoons Ginger Cilantro Pesto (see recipe below)

I pound brie cheese in wheel shape

3 tablespoons grated Parmesan cheese

I tablespoon soft butter

1/4 cup finely chopped macadamia nuts

Hot peppers to taste (optional)

* Experience the flavor of this brie by offering it as a buffet dish rather than a actual serving. Serve with lots of fresh vegetables or even seedless grapes. Limit crackers because they are generally very high in Calories. Think of crackers as mini-dried slices of bread.

Cut brie wheel horizontally through middle so that the wheel resembles two flat discs. Spread pesto on bottom half and sprinkle with Parmesan cheese. If desired, mince hot peppers and sprinkle over Parmesan cheese.

Place top half of brie wheel over pesto and spread top with soft butter. Sprinkle with chopped macadamia nuts.

Serve with crackers and vegetables of your choice.

Ginger Cilantro Pesto

1/4 cup peeled and minced fresh ginger

5 cloves minced fresh garlic

I cup finely chopped cilantro

1/4 cup chopped green onion

1/2 cup salad oil

I teaspoon salt

1/2 teaspoon white pepper

Makes about 1 cup

In a large bowl, combine all ingredients and mix thoroughly. Let pesto sit for 15 minutes before using.

Salmon Spread

This is a quick and easy spread for fancy bread or crackers. Adding a touch of liquid smoke gives simple canned salmon a "fresh from the Northwest" taste.

1 pound canned salmon
8 ounces cream cheese
1/2 cup chopped macadamia nuts
1-1/2 tablespoons minced green onions
1 tablespoon lemon juice
1/4 teaspoon liquid smoke

Combine all ingredients and mix until well blended. Serve with crackers.

* Substitute low-fat cream cheese for full-fat cream cheese to lower total fat by 3 grams and 20 Calories per tablespoon. Do not use non-fat cream cheese, because it alters the flavor.

Hibachi Tofu

Serves 4

Tofu is so versatile. It becomes something different in every dish. Start with firm block tofu. Chill it to make it more firm. When it comes off the grill it will have a great spicy crunch.

1 teaspoon chopped fresh garlic
1/4 teaspoon ground black pepper
1/4 teaspoon chili sauce
1 teaspoon chopped fresh cilantro
1 teaspoon chopped fresh basil
1 tablespoon salad oil
1 teaspoon sesame oil
1/4 teaspoon soy sauce
1 block (20-ounces) firm tofu, drained

Heat coals in a hibachi or barbecue grill. Meanwhile, in a medium size bowl, mix together all ingredients, except tofu. Slice tofu into 4 sections and coat with marinade. Set aside in the refrigerator for about 30 minutes.

When coals are hot, grill tofu until crispy, but not burnt.

Shang Hai Chicken

Serves 4

*It's a party bacon wrap for the cilantro flavored chicken.
Fresh ginger, combined with the Sam Choy creamy oriental dressing,
adds a Chinese flavored zest.*

2 cups soy sauce
1/2 cup vinegar
1/2 cup granulated sugar
1-inch piece fresh ginger, peeled and crushed
1/2 clove fresh garlic
1/2 teaspoon sesame oil
1/2 cup scallions or green onions
1/4 bunch cilantro
1/2 pound bacon
1/4 cup Sam Choy's Creamy Oriental Dressing
2 pounds chicken breast, cut into bite-size pieces
Vegetable oil for deep-frying

In a medium bowl, combine soy sauce, vinegar, sugar, ginger, garlic, sesame oil, green onions, and cilantro. Mix thoroughly. Coat the chicken with sauce and marinate overnight in the refrigerator.

Heat 2-1/2 to 3 inches of oil in a wok or a deep heavy pot over medium-high heat until it registers 350 to 375°F on a deep-fry thermometer.

Wrap each chicken piece with 1/3-slice of bacon and secure bacon with a toothpick. Fry chicken pieces, a few at a time, for 3 to 4 minutes, or until golden brown. Serve with Sam Choy's Creamy Oriental Dressing or your choice of dipping sauce.

* Use skinless chicken breast to decrease the total fat by at least 10 grams and 90 Calories per serving.

GALLO *of* SONOMA
DRY CREEK VALLEY
Zinfandel
BARREL AGED   *1997*

Deep-Fried Won Ton Brie with Fresh Pineapple Marmalade

Serving amount varies

Fry the won ton until it is extra-crisp. Bite in and taste the melted brie, combined with the taste of macadamia nuts. It only gets better when dipped in homemade marmalade.

Pineapple Marmalade (see recipe below)
Won ton wrappers
Brie cheese
Oil for deep-frying

Take a won ton wrapper and brush with egg white. Place a cube of brie in the middle. (You can add a sprinkle of chopped macadamia nut or other nuts, if you like.) Press the cheese down while gathering up the won ton wrapper to make a little purse, and pinch the wrapper together just above the cheese to seal. The won ton wrapper should fan out a little at the top, with the overall effect being one of a miniature gift-wrapped package.

In a deep heavy pot or wok, heat oil to 350°F.

Deep-fry purses to a golden brown for about 2 to 3 minutes. Drain on paper towels. Serve with warm pineapple marmalade (see Tip).

* Another option is to wrap the brie in phyllo dough and bake in a 350°F. oven for about 10 minutes or until golden brown.

Tip: *For a quick dipping sauce, combine a jar of prepared orange or pineapple marmalade and thin with white wine over low heat for about 5 minutes until the sauce becomes a good consistency for dipping. Spice it up with a pinch of hot chili pepper flakes.*

Pineapple Marmalade

Makes 2 cups

2 cups chopped pineapple (fresh or canned)
1 cup granulated sugar
Pinch of hot chili pepper flakes (optional)

In a heavy saucepan, combine pineapple with sugar. Bring the mixture to a boil and then simmer uncovered until it thickens to a syrupy consistency, stirring occasionally. It will take about 45 minutes for fresh pineapple or less, if you're using canned pineapple.

Teriyaki Roll-Ups

Serves 4

Island marinade, with papaya, garlic, ginger, soy, brown sugar, and sherry, turns the steak butter tender. Now, roll it around the vegetables and grill. No barbecue? A wok will work too.

3/4 cup chopped onions
2 tablespoons minced fresh garlic
2 tablespoons peeled and minced fresh ginger
1 tablespoon brown sugar
1-1/2 cups soy sauce
1 cup water
1/2 papaya, seeded, peeled, and mashed
2 tablespoons sherry
1 pound flank steak (sliced into thin sheets)
2 teaspoons vegetable oil
1/2 cup julienned carrots
1/2 cup julienned green beans
2 tablespoons chopped green onions
1/4 cup julienned red peppers
Salt and pepper to taste

To prepare marinade, combine onions, garlic, ginger, brown sugar, soy sauce, water, papaya, and sherry in a large bowl and mix well. Marinate flank steak overnight in refrigerator.

In a large skillet, sauté remaining vegetables over medium-high heat until al dente. Lay a thin sheet of steak on a clean flat surface (like a plate). Spoon vegetables onto one side of the flank steak, season with salt and pepper. Roll the meat and secure it with toothpicks. Grill meat until cooked.

Tip: *Meat rolls can be grilled in a large hot skillet, a wok, or over a hibachi or barbecue.*

Sautéed Prawns with Pickled Ginger

Serves 4

This one may set off the fire alarm when the shrimp are ready to sauté in the hot oil. You need just a bit of flame when you add the wine, to burn off some of the alcohol— careful here. The tingle-on-the-tongue of pickled ginger is a perfect balance to the honey and black bean glazed prawns.

1 pound prawns or extra jumbo shrimp (16-20 count)

Salt and pepper to taste

2 tablespoons vegetable oil

1 tablespoon dry wine

6 tablespoons honey

2-inch piece lemon grass, peeled and finely chopped

2 tablespoons fish sauce

6 tablespoons hoisin sauce (sweet-spicy soybean-garlic sauce)

2 tablespoons chili garlic sauce

2 teaspoons black bean sauce with garlic

Garnish:

Pickled ginger

Green onions, cut on the bias

To prepare prawns or shrimp, peel and devein. Season prawns with salt and pepper.

Heat oil in wok over medium-high heat. Sauté prawns until halfway cooked. Add wine and flame off alcohol. Add honey, lemon grass, and the remaining sauces. Simmer until prawns are glazed.

Place prawns on individual plates or present them on a platter and top with pickled ginger and green onions.

* In place of 2 tablespoons vegetable oil, use 1 teaspoon vegetable oil and a non-stick wok to decrease total fat by 6 grams and 50 Calories per serving.

Thai Style Shrimp Rolls

Serves 4

Tied with scallions, these shrimp rolls may take some time to prepare but the festive look, and perfect match with the peanut dipping sauce, make them a party favorite.

Dipping Sauce (see recipe below)
I pound extra jumbo shrimp (16 to 20 count), peeled and deveined
16 to 20 sheets small square rice paper
I cucumber, seeded and cut into 3-inch strips (16 to 20 strips)
16 to 20 sprigs of fresh cilantro
Fresh basil and mint leaves (I to 2 each per roll)
1/2 bunch scallions or green onion (16 to 20 stems)

In a large saucepan, bring 3-inches of water to a boil. Add shrimp to liquid. As soon as water returns to a boil, remove shrimp (Do not overcook). Retain water for blanching scallions.

Assemble shrimp rolls by first dipping each sheet of rice paper in warm water for a few seconds to soften. Then place a shrimp, cucumber slice, cilantro sprig, basil leaf, and mint leaf diagonally in the rice paper. Fold over the bottom corner to cover greens and proceed to roll into tubes. Let leaves hang out the edge.

Blanch scallions and use them to tie around the rice paper. Serve on a platter with dipping sauce on the side.

Dipping Sauce

2 tablespoons chunky peanut butter
1/4 cup soy sauce
3 tablespoons vinegar
2 tablespoons hoisin sauce (sweet-spicy soybean-garlic sauce)
2 tablespoons lime juice
1/8 teaspoon red chili pepper flakes

Makes about 3/4 cup

Combine and blend ingredients together.

Drunken Shrimp

Serves 4

No worry, I tell the parents, even the kids can have these.
Most of the alcohol cooks away, leaving just the Tequila tingle.
They are great on the hibachi, but if you're tailgating
watch out, the aroma draws a crowd!

**Drunken Shrimp Marinade
(see recipe below)**

16 whole extra jumbo shrimp (16 to 20 count), peeled and deveined

Heat coals in a hibachi or barbecue grill. Meanwhile marinate shrimp for 30 minutes. When coals are hot, grill for about 1 to 1-1/2 minutes per side. Serve with steamed rice.

Tip: *If cooking shrimp in a wok or skillet, after removing the shrimp you should deglaze the pan with any remaining marinade or white wine. This last minute sauce is worth every last drop.*

Drunken Shrimp Marinade

Makes about 2/3 cup

**3 shots Cabo Wabo Tequila
(about 6 tablespoons)**

**Lime juice from 4 limes
(about 4 tablespoons)**

3 jalapeño peppers, chopped

1 tablespoon chopped fresh garlic

**1 teaspoon cayenne pepper
or to taste**

Salt and pepper to taste

Combine and mix well.

Tip: *Chili garlic paste may be substituted for fresh garlic and jalapeño pepper.*

Corn Battered Shrimp with Tartar Sauce

Serves 4

Just a bit of Creole seasoning, some Creole Tartar Sauce for dipping, and the Corn Masque Choux and you have a Cajun table. Shrimp cook quickly. Over-cook and you have a great batter on rubber shrimp.

Creole Tartar Sauce (see page 13)

1 large ear corn (for 1/2 cup corn kernels and additional corn milk)

1 egg

2 cups milk

2 teaspoons Creole seasoning

1/2 teaspoon baking soda

3/4 cup yellow corn meal

1/4 cup all-purpose flour

1/4 teaspoon salt

1/4 teaspoon freshly ground black pepper

16 extra jumbo shrimp, (16 to 20 count) peeled, deveined and butterflied

Vegetable oil for deep-frying

Hold the ear of corn and thinly slice across the top of corn kernels. Then cut across the kernels a second time to release the milk. Scrape the cob once or twice to extract the milk.

In a bowl, whip together egg, milk, 1 teaspoon Creole seasoning, corn kernels and corn milk until smooth, about 1 minute. Blend in baking soda, corn meal, flour, salt and black pepper. Mix well to make a thick batter.

Prepare deep-fryer by heating oil to 375°F as measured by a deep-fry thermometer. Season shrimp with remaining 1 teaspoon Creole seasoning. Dip each shrimp in batter to coat evenly. Fry 3 shrimp at a time until golden brown. Drain on paper towels.

Serve immediately along with Creole Tartar Sauce for dipping and Corn Masque Choux (see page 13).

* Creole Tartar Sauce is both flavorful and high-fat. You only need to use only a little sauce for a lot of flavor.

Creole Tartar Sauce

I egg
1 tablespoon minced fresh garlic
2 tablespoons fresh lemon juice
1 tablespoon chopped fresh parsley
2 tablespoons chopped green onions
1 cup olive oil
1/8 teaspoon cayenne pepper
1 tablespoon whole grain mustard
1 teaspoon salt

Makes 1-1/2 cups

Combine egg, garlic, lemon juice, parsley and green onions in a food processor and puree for 15 seconds. With the processor running, pour olive oil slowly through the feeding tube in a steady stream. Tap in cayenne pepper, mustard and salt. Pulse once or twice to blend. Cover sauce and refrigerate for 1 hour before using. Sauce is best used within 24 hours.

Corn Masque Choux

6 ears young corn (to make 4 cups of corn with corn milk)
2 tablespoons vegetable oil
1 cup diced onions
1/2 cup diced green bell peppers
1-1/2 teaspoon salt
1/4 teaspoon cayenne pepper
1 cup chopped, peeled, and seeded tomatoes (or chopped canned tomatoes)
1/2 cup milk

Makes 7 cups

Holding each ear of corn, thinly slice across the top of corn kernels and then cut across the kernels a second time to release the milk. Scrape the cob once or twice to extract the milk.

Heat oil in a wok or large skillet over medium-high heat. Season onions and bell peppers with salt and cayenne pepper. To the wok, add seasoned vegetables, corn, and tomatoes. Cook for about 15 minutes or until corn is tender. Stir occasionally. Add milk, stir and remove from the heat. Serve immediately.

* Use only 1 teaspoon oil to decrease total fat by 3 grams and 20 Calories per cup.

Oyster Poor Boy | *Serves 4*

You can make his "house" into his serving dish with a thorough scrub, but that dish will be empty in no time. Spicy golden brown oysters are always a smash hit.

8 fresh large oysters, shucked (see Note)
Peanut oil for frying
1/4 cup all-purpose flour
1/4 cup cornmeal
1/2 teaspoon Tabasco sauce
Cajun spice to taste
Pinch of white pepper

Drain the oysters of their liquid and lay them on paper towels to dry.

Heat 2-1/2 to 3 inches of oil in a wok or heavy pot over medium-high heat until it registers 375°F on a deep-fry thermometer. Preheat oven to 200°F

In a shallow bowl, combine flour and cornmeal. Season oysters with Tabasco, Cajun spice, and white pepper. Coat seasoned oysters with flour-cornmeal mix, shaking off excess coating.

Fry 4 oysters until golden brown (2 to 3 minutes); drain on paper towels. Allow the oil to return to 375°F before adding the second batch of oysters. Place the fried oysters in a 200°F oven to keep warm until all oysters are fried and ready to serve.

Note: *If bottom shells are desired for presentation, shells should be thoroughly scrubbed under cold running water.*

Baked Lu'au Oysters

Serves 4

If you look at a platter of oysters on the half shell you may see elegance. Or, you may see a raw oyster looking back. To savor the flavor add a bit of Egg Lu'au Sauce and broil them brown. Then see how fast they go down.

Egg Lu'au Sauce (see recipe below)
12 oysters, on a half shell (see Note)
1 teaspoon peeled and minced fresh ginger
1 teaspoon minced fresh garlic
1 teaspoon finely chopped fresh cilantro
1 tablespoon chopped green onions

Preheat broiler for 5 minutes.

Arrange oysters on a platter that can be placed in an oven. Sprinkle oysters with ginger, garlic, cilantro and green onions. Cover each oyster with Egg Lu'au Sauce. Place oysters under the broiler for a couple of minutes or until the tops are brown. These oysters are now ready to enjoy!

Egg Lu'au Sauce

Makes 3/4 cup

2 tablespoons blanched lu'au leaf (young taro leaf), or spinach leaves
3 eggs
1 tablespoon white wine
Salt and white pepper to taste

To blanch lu'au leaf, remove stem from lu'au leaf and blanch in boiling water for 3 minutes. Strain in colander. Set aside.

Heat water in the bottom of a double boiler. Whip eggs and white wine together. Pour egg mixture in the top of double boiler. Cook while stirring constantly. Add salt and white pepper to taste. When egg mixture is a taffy consistency, stir in the cooked lu'au leaves. Pour into a cup.

Note: *Under cold running water, use a brush to scrub all of the dirt from the oyster shell. With a towel, hold the oyster with one hand while inserting the point of a blunt knife into the hinge of the shell. Twist the knife until the shell pops open. Use the knife tip to loosen the oyster meat. Rinse under cold running water*

Steamed Clams with Chili and Ginger Pesto Butter

Serves 4

The delicate flavor of small steamer clams is beautifully balanced by the Asian flavors of the kai choy mustard cabbage and shiitake mushrooms. After the clams are steamed and in their bowls, top them with the chili, garlic, chili butter, and the Ginger Pesto Butter. If there is any left, the ginger pesto can be refrigerated and used on a pasta dish or as a spread.

4 tablespoons **Chili Butter**
(see recipe below)

4 tablespoons **Ginger Pesto Butter**
(see recipe on page 17)

24 **steamer clams**

1/2 cup **chicken stock** or
low-sodium chicken broth

1/2 teaspoon **chopped fresh garlic**

1/2 cup **rinsed and julienned
fresh shiitake mushrooms**

1/2 cup **julienned kai choy
(mustard cabbage)**

1/2 cup **sliced round onions**

2 tablespoons **chopped green onion**

1/2 cup **dry white wine**

Scrub clams under cold running water with a brush before opening them. Insert a blunt knife between the shell's two halves and twist the knife slightly to open the shell. Again use the knife to gently release the clam from its shell.

In a small pot, bring chicken stock to a strong boil. Add clams and chopped garlic. Steam for 1 minute. Add all vegetables for about 3 minutes. Remove from stove.

Divide between 4 serving bowls. Top each bowl with 1 tablespoon chili butter and 1 tablespoon ginger pesto butter.

Chili Butter

2 tablespoons **chili garlic paste**
1 stick (1/4 pound) **softened butter**
1 **Hawaiian chili pepper**, minced
Salt and pepper to taste

Makes 5/8 cup

Blend all ingredients together thoroughly.

Ginger Pesto Butter

**2 tablespoons Ginger Pesto
(see recipe below)**
I stick (1/4 pound) softened butter

Makes 1/2 cup

Blend ginger pesto with butter until pesto is
evenly distributed.

Ginger Pesto

**1/4 cup peeled and minced
fresh ginger**
1/2 cup chopped green onions
**8 fresh peeled garlic cloves
(about 1 ounce)**
1/4 cup fresh cilantro
I cup salad oil (like canola oil)
Salt and pepper to taste

Makes about 1-3/4 cups

Combine ginger, green onions, garlic, cilantro and
salt and pepper in a food processor and puree for
15 seconds. With the processor running, pour
salad oil slowly through the feeding tube in a
steady stream. When well blended, this can be
used immediately or refrigerated for later use.

Breaded Oysters with Wasabi Cocktail Sauce

Serves 4

*Wasabi powder in the coating mix and wasabi paste in the sauce
give the zip of Japanese horseradish to these golden brown deep-fried oysters.
They take three minutes to cook and even less to eat.*

**Wasabi Cocktail Sauce
(see recipe below)**

**12 oysters, shucked
(see Note on page 15)**

1 cup all-purpose flour

1 tablespoon wasabi powder

1 tablespoon curry powder

Salt and pepper to taste

4 eggs, whipped

**4 cups panko (Japanese-style
crispy bread crumbs) or fine
dried bread crumbs**

**2 cups vegetable oil for
deep-frying**

Drain the oysters of their liquid and lay them on paper towels to dry. In a shallow bowl, mix flour, wasabi powder, curry powder, and salt and pepper until thoroughly blended. In a second bowl, whip the eggs. Pour panko into a third shallow bowl.

Heat 2-1/2 to 3-inches of oil in a wok or deep heavy pot over medium-high heat until it sizzles. Meanwhile, coat oysters with flour mixture, shaking off excess. Then dip oysters into whipped eggs and rolled them in panko. Set aside until all oysters are breaded and oil registers 375°F on a deep-fry thermometer.

Fry oysters a few at a time for 2 or 3 minutes or until golden brown. Drain briefly on paper towels. Allow oil to return to 375°F before adding new batch of oysters. Serve with Wasabi Cocktail Sauce.

Wasabi Cocktail Sauce

Makes 3/4 cup

**1 tablespoon wasabi paste
(Japanese horseradish)**

1 teaspoon water

1/4 teaspoon soy sauce

1/4 cup ketchup

1/2 cup chili sauce

Salt and pepper to taste

In a small bowl mix wasabi paste, water, and soy sauce into a smooth paste. Blend wasabi-soy sauce mixture with ketchup, chili sauce, and salt and pepper.

* Make sure that deep-fry oil is appropriately hot, so that the oysters absorb minimum fat.

Oven-Roasted Dungeness Crab with Garlic Butter

Serves 4

When it comes to eating crab, butter is the way to go. Add in garlic and you are getting close to Paradise. Now, pack the crab's shell and bake and you have food for the gods.

1 large Kona Gold Dungeness crab or Dungeness crab
1 stick (1/4 pound) softened butter
2 tablespoons minced fresh garlic
1 tablespoon chopped fresh cilantro
1 teaspoon chili pepper flakes
Juice from 1 lemon (about 2 tablespoons)
Pinch of salt and pepper

Preheat oven to 375°F

To clean a crab, hold the legs down with the right hand while griping the head of the crab from underneath with the left hand. With even pressure, pull the "helmet" off the crab. Remove gills and mouth.

Mix butter, garlic, cilantro, chili pepper, lemon juice, salt, and pepper. Pack herb butter into crab (under shell and all around). Place stuffed crab into a baking pan and cover with foil. Bake for about 15 minutes.

Lobster Crab Dip for Asparagus

Makes about 7 cups dip

When you are looking for true extravagance in taste, this is it.
To the blend of lobster, crab meat, and al dente asparagus spears we
add dill and curry. The result is beyond description.

3 gallons boiling water, or enough
to cover lobsters

4 tablespoons Hawaiian salt

2 lobster tails

large bowl of ice water

1-1/2 cups mayonnaise

1/2 pound of cooked crabmeat

1 pound frozen mixed vegetables
(mix of corn, carrot, and peas)

1-1/2 cup rinsed and chopped
fresh spinach

Juice of 2 lemons
(about 4 tablespoons)

2 tablespoon chopped dill weed

1/3 teaspoon curry powder

1/3 teaspoon white pepper

Salt to taste

2 pound fresh asparagus

In a large pot, bring water and salt to a boil. Immerse whole lobster into boiling water for approximately 8 minutes. Using tongs, carefully remove lobster from water and immediately submerge tails into a large bowl of ice water. When completely cooled, remove lobster from shell and cut lobster into small pieces.

Meanwhile, blanch frozen mixed vegetables for 3 minutes in rapidly boiling water. Strain and cool. Toss mixed vegetables, mayonnaise, crabmeat, and lobster with spinach, lemon juice, and seasonings. Mix thoroughly and chill until ready to serve.

Wash asparagus and snap or trim off tough ends (generally where it breaks easily). Remove lower scales or peel bottom if desired. Submerge asparagus in boiling water. Simmer until the asparagus is just tender.

Arrange asparagus on platter and serve with chilled lobster dip.

* In place of 1-1/2 cups mayonnaise, use 1/2 cup mayonnaise and 1 cup non-fat mayonnaise to decrease the total fat by more than half, yet maintain the flavor.

Crab Rangoon

Makes about 72 won ton

The edible flowers give a confetti look to these crispy, cheesy, crab pupu. Don't crowd the pan when you deep fry and the result will be a platter of perfect, golden won ton.

12 ounces cream cheese, softened

6 ounces grated Swiss cheese (about 1-1/2 cups)

3 tablespoons granulated sugar

1/8 teaspoon curry powder

1/3 teaspoon salt

1 teaspoon sesame oil

1 teaspoon hot sauce

1/2 teaspoon minced fresh garlic

1/2 teaspoon peeled and minced fresh ginger

won ton pi (4- by 4-inch size)

1 pound cooked crabmeat, diced

1/8 cup edible flowers (pansies or nasturtiums)

Water (to dampen won ton edges)

Vegetable oil for deep-frying

Using a fork, blend cream cheese and grated Swiss cheese together until smooth. Thoroughly mix in all the seasonings. Add crabmeat and edible flowers if desired and blend enough to evenly distributed.

Place one small dot of crab-mixture in center of won ton pi. Dampen the edges of the won ton with water and fold each edge upward to form a small pouch.

Heat 2-1/2 to 3 inches of oil in a wok (or a deep heavy pot) over medium high heat until it registers 350°F on a deep-fry thermometer. Deep-fry crab won ton pi, a few at a time, until golden brown. Remove and drain on paper towels.

GALLO *of* SONOMA
RUSSIAN RIVER VALLEY
Chardonnay
BARREL FERMENTED   *1998*

Philadelphia Fish and Company's Award-Winning

Philly Crab Cakes with Curry Aioli

Serves 6

*It's that "butter is better" thing again.
These crab cakes come golden brown in clarified butter.
Surrounded by an Asian flavored Aioli, they do
melt in the mouth.*

Curry Aioli (see recipe on page 25)
1 pound cooked crabmeat (snow or lump crab is recommended)
1 teaspoon Worcestershire sauce
1 dash Tabasco
1 tablespoon finely chopped ogo seaweed
1 teaspoon curry powder
1 teaspoon dry mustard
1 teaspoon Philly Magic (see Note 1)
1 tablespoon chopped scallions or green onions
1 tablespoon diced red bell pepper
1 cup dry bread crumbs
1/4 cup mayonnaise
Salt and pepper to taste
1/2 cup all-purpose flour
1/2 cup clarified butter (see Note 2)

Mix together Worcestershire sauce, Tabasco, ogo, curry powder, dry mustard, Philly Magic, scallions, red peppers, and mayonnaise. Fold these ingredients, along with bread crumbs into crab meat and mix thoroughly. Form into 6 patties, about 4 ounces each. Place the flour on a plate and lightly coat the crab cakes.

Heat clarified butter in a sauté pan over medium heat. Pan fry crab cakes until brown (about 1-1/2 minutes per side).

Arrange fish cakes on platter and serve with Curry Aioli.

Note 1: *Philly Magic (equal amounts of garlic powder, onion powder, Old Bay Seasoning, paprika, and cayenne)*

Note 2: *To clarify butter, slowly melt unsalted butter until water evaporates and milk solids sink to the bottom of the pan. Skim foam off the top and pour off clear (clarified) butter.*

* Make up mayonnaise blend as described in Curry Aioli as the first step to lower fat and Calories and then limit the clarified butter to 4 tablespoons or less.

Curry Aioli

1/2 cup mayonnaise
1/4 cup chopped cilantro
1 teaspoon minced fresh garlic
1 tablespoon rice wine vinegar
1 teaspoon fresh lime juice
1 teaspoon curry powder
1 teaspoon sesame oil
Salt and pepper to taste

Makes 3/4 cup

Combine all ingredients in a bowl and mix thoroughly.

* In place of 1/2 cup mayonnaise, use 3 tablespoons mayonnaise and 5 tablespoons non-fat mayonnaise to decrease the total fat by more than half.

Asian-Style Poke

Makes 7 cups

Seven cups sounds like a lot, until the first taste.
Depending on how much chili pepper flakes you use, this traditional poke
can be warm, warmer or pretty hot. A cup of fresh poi and
a cool drink are a perfect balance.

2 pounds very fresh 'ahi (yellowfin tuna), cut into 1/4- to 3/8-inch cubes

1 cup rinsed and chopped ogo seaweed

1/3 cup finely chopped onions

1/4 cup furikake (dried seaweed flakes blended with sesame seeds and seasoning)

2 tablespoons sesame oil

1 tablespoon balsamic vinegar

1 tablespoon granulated sugar

1 tablespoon soy sauce

1 tablespoon chopped green onions

1/2 teaspoon red chili pepper flakes

Combine all ingredients and mix well. Refrigerate until ready to serve.

Sam-Style Poke

Serves 8

*Thousands of entries in the Sam Choy / Aloha Festivals
Poke Recipe Contest and thousands of orders for the many kinds of poke we
serve at the restaurants shows me that poke is finally going mainstream.*

**2/3 cup Sam's Secret Sauce
(see recipe below)**

**2 pounds finely diced 'ahi
(yellowfin tuna)**

4 teaspoons 'inamona (see Note)

**I cup rinsed and chopped
ogo seaweed**

I tablespoon sesame oil

I teaspoon soy sauce

Combine 'ahi with 'inamona, ogo, sesame oil, and soy sauce. Mix thoroughly. Add Sam's secret sauce and marinate for 30 to 60 minutes in the refrigerator. Enjoy.

Sam's Secret Sauce

Makes 2 cups

2 cups water

2 tablespoons Hawaiian salt

**2 Hawaiian chili peppers,
finely chopped**

Combine ingredients and stir until salt completely dissolves.

Note: *'Inamona is a mash of roasted, salted kukui nut. Roasted salted cashew nuts can be substituted if kukui not is not available.*

Fried Poke

Makes about 2 cups

The firmness of swordfish is perfect for a quick-fry poke. Searing it fast seals in the flavor and moisture. You have to use this technique carefully. If you don't remove the fish quickly from the hot pan, it will overcook. Basically, you just slap the fish in the pan, sizzle it on all sides and take it right back out.

7 ounces swordfish cut into 1/2-inch cubes

1/3 cup medium diced white onions

1/3 cup sliced green onions

1/2 cup rinsed and chopped ogo seaweed

1-1/2 tablespoons soy sauce

1/2 teaspoon Hawaiian salt

3 drops sesame oil

Sam Choy's Big Aloha Beer or other beer (optional marinade)

Heat wok to medium-high. Combine all ingredients, except beer, in a bowl and mix well. Quickly fry poke in wok and set aside. Marinate with beer to taste if desired.

Hana Hou Poke
7th Annual Sam Choy Poke Festival Winner

Makes about 10 cups

If the taste and texture of opihi is new to you, this dish is a perfect introduction. Combined with the light aku and the salty 'inamona mash it is easy to taste the reason for the "hana hou—do it again" name. The first bite tastes 'ono.

2 pounds fresh aku (skipjack tuna)

1-1/2 tablespoons Hawaiian salt with 'inamona (see Note)

1 cup rinsed and chopped limu kohu (soft seaweed)

3 Hawaiian chili peppers, diced

2 tablespoons light soy sauce

2 cups 'opihi (25-cent size 'opihi)

1/4 cup Hawaiian salt

1 cup chopped green onions

10 cherry tomatoes, sliced in half

Cut aku into 1/4- to 3/8-inch cubes. Combine aku, Hawaiian salt, limu, chili peppers, and soy sauce. Mix thoroughly and marinate in refrigerator.

Shell 'opihi and rinse with water. Place in colander, add a small handful of Hawaiian salt, squeeze together several times, then rinse under running water. Add a little more salt and mix. Place colander in a bowl and let drain in refrigerator for 1 hour.

In a large bowl, combine aku and 'opihi and mix in green onions and cherry tomatoes. Enjoy!

Note: *'Inamona is a mash of roasted, salted kukui nut. Substitute 2 tablespoons roasted salted cashew nuts if kukui nut is unavailable.*

I *always get a laugh when I talk about my "Summer Soup... some-a dis and some-a dat." Soup is a comfort food. It tastes like "home." Nothing smells as good as a pot of soup simmering on the stove. But, seriously, just think about tastes that go together. Ingredients that can be friendly in the pot. Soup doesn't have to be hard, it doesn't have to be an all-day deal. Many of my soups are fast, sometimes under ten minutes.*

O*n the show I've prepared simple soups. The recipes are all here. Think about a chilled fruit soup. Cool and light for a hot Hawaiian day. It makes a nice starter if you are serving a rich entrée. Or, a sweet fruit soup can follow the meal, as dessert.*

Salads should be exciting. I like to layer things. Mix things, layer fruit with chicken on greens, try seaweed and fish, raw or seared. Don't be afraid to experiment. Cilantro and mint make a salad taste exotic. Nuts and raisins can mix with chili peppers. Think sweet, tart and spicy at the same time, giving every bite an exciting taste!

A salad can be a whole meal. Think of combining some marinated chicken with fruit, tossed with cold pasta, and surrounded by greens. The preparation time is short. Sam Choy's dressings make it even quicker. Top off your creation with a scattering of edible flowers for an elegant look.

Poha Berry Bisque

Serves 8

*You can freeze any fruit. When they are about to be too ripe,
freeze them and they'll keep until you need them for a dish like this. The color
isn't very good when they come out of the freezer, but the juice and
poha berries or poha preserves will fix that.*

1-1/2 pounds ripened papaya, seeded, peeled and chopped

1 pound ripe mango, seeded and roughly chopped

1/2 cup granulated sugar

2 cups stemmed poha berries (goose berries) (see Note)

2 cups pineapple juice

3 or 4 black peppercorns

1/2 cinnamon stick or 1 teaspoon ground cinnamon

1/4 teaspoon allspice

Garnish:

Dollop of sour cream

Sprinkle with chopped toasted macadamia nuts

Cinnamon stick (optional)

In a large saucepan, combine papaya, mango, sugar, poha berries, pineapple juice, black peppercorns, cinnamon stick and allspice. Stir over low heat, stirring constantly until blended and sugar has dissolved.

Serve in bowls and garnish with a dollop of sour cream and sprinkle with chopped toasted macadamia nuts. If desired, add visually with a cinnamon stick.

Note: *1-1/2 cups of poha preserves can be substituted for fresh poha berries, however, decrease sugar to 1/8 cup.*

Papaya, Mint & Coconut Soup

Serves 4

Nothing like a cool soup on a hot Hawaiian day. Ripe papayas and coconut milk make this rich and creamy. You can leave out the rum when the kids are eating.

2 medium sized ripe papayas, peeled, seeded and chopped

2 cups coconut milk

2 tablespoons dark rum (optional)

2 tablespoons mint leaves

2 teaspoons honey

1 teaspoon island seasoning (nutmeg, cinnamon, thyme, allspice)

Garnish:

Sprigs of mint

Place the papayas, coconut milk, rum (optional), mint leaves, honey, and island seasoning in a food processor. Puree for 20 to 30 seconds or until mixture is smooth. Refrigerate 1 hour before serving. Garnish with a sprig of mint.

* By substituting a low-fat coconut milk for the regular coconut milk, for each serving you can lower total fat by 5 grams and Calories by 50.

Winter Pumpkin Soup

Serves 4 to 5

*Too many people think pumpkins are only for carving or for pie.
This soup is even better when you add the sweet potato. The heavy cream
and butter at the end add the smoothness. Don't forget the thick slices of bread
or your family may just lick the bowl.*

1 pumpkin (about 4 pounds)
2 sweet potatoes (optional)
2 large onions, chopped
1/4 cup olive oil
2 cups water
2 cups whole milk
**Salt and freshly ground black pepper,
to taste (about a pinch of each)**
4 teaspoons granulated sugar
1/2 cup heavy cream
3 tablespoons unsalted butter

Garnish:

**4 thick slices toasted or grilled
country bread or sourdough bread**

Peel the pumpkin, remove seeds and fibers, and cut into chunks. Peel and wash the optional sweet potato and cut into chunks.

In a large heavy saucepan, cook the onion in the olive oil until golden. Add the pumpkin and sweet potato. Cook over very low heat for 5 minutes, stirring frequently with a wooden spoon to prevent sticking.

Add water and milk. (If this does not cover the vegetables, add enough water and milk to do so). Add the salt, freshly ground black pepper, and sugar and stir. Cook for 30 minutes over low heat. Add the heavy cream and butter. Bring to a boil for 1 minute.

Serve immediately garnished with thick slices of toasted or grilled country bread.

Portuguese Sausage Corn Soup

Serves 6 to 8

*If you have fresh corn to cut off the cob, it's great.
But frozen or canned corn works fine when you blend the
Portuguese sausage, garlic, fresh vegetables and Creole seasonings.
Never plan for leftovers, there won't be any.*

1 tablespoon salad oil

1 cup medium diced onions

1 cup medium diced celery

**1 cup medium diced
green bell pepper**

**2 tablespoons minced
fresh garlic**

2 cups minced Portuguese sausage

**3 cups corn kernels (frozen
or canned may be used)**

2 tablespoons unsalted butter

1/4 cup all-purpose flour

3/4 gallon water

**1 cup chicken stock or
low-sodium chicken broth**

**2 tablespoons Creole seasoning
(see Note)**

2 tablespoons granulated sugar

Pinch of salt and pepper

In a sauce pan or wok, heat salad oil on medium heat. Add onions, celery, bell peppers, and garlic and cook for 3 to 4 minutes or until onions are translucent. Add Portuguese sausage and corn, cook for about 2 to 3 minutes, constantly stirring so mixture does not burn. Add butter to the mixture until melted then gradually add the flour to thicken mixture. Add water gradually while constantly stirring in chicken stock. Season with Creole spice, sugar and salt and pepper to taste. Simmer for 1 hour; then serve.

Note: *Creole spice may be purchased in the condiment section of your favorite grocery store.*

GALLO *of* SONOMA
DRY CREEK VALLEY
Zinfandel

BARREL AGED   *1997*

ALC. 14.5% BY VOL.

Tahitian Crabmeat Soup

Serves 6 to 8

*The heavy cream, crab meat and coconut milk
give this soup a Tahitian look and flavor. Be sure to use the white pepper.
Black pepper will make it look like the spinach wasn't washed clean.*

2 cups medium diced onion

1/4 cup unsalted butter

2 tablespoons all-purpose flour

2 cups heavy cream

**1-1/2 cups chicken stock or
low-sodium chicken broth**

2 cups coconut milk

**2 cups frozen chopped spinach
(thawed) or 3 cups chopped
fresh spinach**

1-1/2 cups crabmeat

Salt and white pepper to taste

In a large saucepan, sauté onion in butter until translucent on low heat. Stir in flour and blend well. Add heavy cream and chicken stock. Simmer for 5 minutes, stirring frequently. Add coconut milk, spinach and crabmeat. Cook for 5 more minutes stirring frequently. Season to taste with salt and white pepper.

Serve immediately.

* Use a low-fat coconut milk for the regular coconut milk to lower the total fat and Calories without changing the taste. Also you can cut the recipe in half and serve smaller portions.

Teriyaki Tofu Bean Salad

Serves 4

*Tofu is so versatile, you can do many dishes with it.
You can even substitute tofu for meats. Here we fry cubes of firm tofu
until it is golden brown and then mix it into a salad of beans and greens.
Then it all gets dressed in a tangy Teriyaki Vinaigrette.*

**Teriyaki Vinaigrette
(see recipe on page 39)**

I pound firm tofu cut

Cornstarch for dusting

2 tablespoons peanut oil

**2 cups rinsed and sliced
fresh shiitake mushrooms**

I tomato, seeded and sliced

**I can (15 ounces) garbanzo
beans, drained**

I green pepper, seeded and diced

1/4 cup diced onions

I teaspoon chopped fresh cilantro

**2 teaspoons peeled and minced
fresh ginger**

White pepper to taste

**Mixed island greens, rinse and torn
(if necessary) into bite-size pieces**

Garnish:

**3 tablespoons chopped
unsalted almonds**

Sliced cucumbers

Cut firm tofu into cubes and drain. Dust in cornstarch and shake off any excess. In a wok, heat peanut oil to medium-high and fry tofu cubes until brown.

Mix together: shiitake mushrooms, tomatoes, garbanzo beans, diced green pepper, onions, Cilantro, ginger, and white pepper. Toss Teriyaki Vinaigrette with bean mixture.

On individual plates, place the bean mixture on top of a bed of mixed salad greens. Add fried tofu and garnish with almonds and cucumbers. Serve immediately.

* Substitute the regular firm tofu with extra firm low-fat silken-type tofu to decrease 7.5 grams total fat and 95 calories per serving.

Teriyaki Vinaigrette

1/2 cup soy sauce

1/4 cup granulated sugar

1/2 teaspoon peeled and minced
fresh ginger

2 teaspoons Dijon mustard

1 tablespoon sliced fresh garlic

1/4 cup balsamic vinegar

1/4 cup olive oil

1/2 teaspoon white pepper

1/2 teaspoon granulated sugar

1/2 teaspoon pepper flakes

1 tablespoon black goma seeds
(sesame seeds)

Makes 1 cup

In a large bowl, combine all ingredients for
the vinaigrette. Stir until sugar is dissolved.

Crispy Scallop Salad

Serves 6

*These shellfish add a delicate but powerful flavor to salad.
Prepared in the poaching liquid, they are zesty and melt in the mouth,
all at the same time. The addition of a sliced apple complements
the diverse combination of other ingredients.*

1-1/2 pounds scallops

**Scallop Poaching Liquid
(see recipe below)**

1/2 cup lime juice

1/3 cup olive oil

1/3 cup granulated sugar

1 clove fresh garlic, sliced

1 tablespoon minced fresh tarragon

1 teaspoon salt

1-1/2 cups fresh celery, sliced
diagonally

6 cups Waimea mixed salad greens or any
mixed lettuce of your choice

3/4 cup sliced red radish

2 medium tomatoes,
cut into wedges

1 Asian apple, julienned
(such as Fuji apple)

1-1/2 cups julienned jicama

Rinse scallops in cold running water and drain well. In a large saucepan, bring poaching liquid to a rapid boil. Add scallops and reduce the heat. Simmer scallops for 3 to 5 minutes, or until scallops are tender. Drain scallops.

Combine: lime juice, oil, sugar, garlic, tarragon, and salt. Pour over scallops, cover and chill for several hours. Add celery and mix. Drain, but save marinade.

Arrange mixed greens evenly on six salad plates. Divide scallops and celery mixture evenly between plates. Arrange the remaining foods in groups around the scallops on the mixed greens. Serve with reserved marinade.

Scallop Poaching Liquid

4 cups boiling water

1/2 cup white wine

1/2 tablespoon tarragon

1-1/2 teaspoons salt and pepper mix

1/2 tablespoon peppercorns, cracked

2 cups diced mirepoix
(onion, carrots, and celery)

1 stem fresh cilantro

Combine ingredients.

Ogo Salad

Serves 4

Ogo seaweed is a mainstay ingredient in preparing poke.
Many folks think of it only as a garnish. The flavor of fresh ogo
seems like a crunchy taste of the ocean itself.

6 tablespoons balsamic vinegar
2 tablespoons granulated sugar
I teaspoon red pepper chili flakes
4 cups fresh ogo seaweed (mixed)
1/2 cup julienned onions
I cup chopped fresh tomatoes

In a medium-size bowl, combine vinegar, sugar, and chili flakes until sugar is dissolved. Set aside.

Rinse and chop ogo. Add ogo and remaining ingredients to vinegar mix. Toss salad ingredients together. Enjoy!

Bean Sprout Salad

Serves 4

The simple bean sprout goes up-town with a local style
dressing and fresh toasted sesame seeds.

I pound blanched bean sprouts
(see Note)
5 tablespoons white sesame seeds
4-1/2 tablespoons vinegar
I teaspoon salt
2 teaspoons soy sauce
2 tablespoons granulated sugar
I teaspoon sesame oil
6 tablespoons chopped
fresh cilantro
6 stalks green onions, minced

Garnish:
Additional toasted sesame seeds

Prepare dressing by combining vinegar, salt, soy sauce, sugar, and sesame oil in a bowl. Whisk until thoroughly combined.

To toast white sesame seeds, brown them slowly over low heat in a covered pan. Mix together green onions, cilantro, and bean sprouts and coat with dressing.

Garnish with additional toasted sesame seeds, if desired.

Note: *Partially fill a 3-quart pot with water, leaving enough room to submerge sprouts without overflowing the pot. Place pot on medium-high heat. Rinse bean sprouts in cold water and when heated water reaches a rapid boil, dip sprouts in water for 30 seconds and strain.*

Fresh Island Sautéed Spinach with Garlic

Serves 6

*Even though this salad is cooked, it is still a salad.
You just add melted butter, fresh garlic, well-washed spinach,
and roasted sesame seeds.*

2 pounds fresh island spinach, washed and large stem ends trimmed

4 tablespoons (1/2 stick) butter

2 tablespoons minced fresh garlic

Salt and pepper to taste

3 tablespoons roasted sesame seeds

In a large wok or sauté pan, heat butter over low to medium heat until melted. Add garlic and stir, being careful not to burn the garlic. Add fresh spinach and sauté until spinach becomes limp.

To serve, spoon onto individual plates or in a "family-style" bowl. Sprinkle roasted sesame seeds on top.

* To decrease total fat by 5 grams and 45 Calories per serving, prepare wok with 5 seconds of butter-flavored vegetable oil spray and then add 1 tablespoon butter just before serving.

Black-Eyed Pea Salad

Serves 4

For some old fashioned Southern good luck, or just because you love the taste of black-eyed peas, serve up this healthy, light salad.

1-1/2 cups dried black-eyed peas
**1/8 teaspoon salt
(for boiling water)**
1/4 cup rice wine vinegar
1/3 cup light olive oil
1/2 cup minced fresh cilantro
1/2 cup minced red onion
Salt and pepper to taste
1 tablespoon canola oil
2 cloves minced fresh garlic
1 red bell pepper, minced

In a large pot, cover black-eyed peas with at least 2-inches of salted cold water; bring peas to a boil. Reduce heat to a simmer and cook until tender, about 45 to 60 minutes. Drain beans and mix them with the rice wine vinegar, olive oil, cilantro, and minced onion. Season to taste with salt and pepper and set aside.

In a large skillet, heat the canola oil over high heat. Quickly stir-fry garlic and bell pepper for about 30 seconds. Add garlic-pepper mixture to beans and toss gently. Serve at room temperature.

Tip: *This is a great dish to serve on New Year's Day. In the South, it is believed that you will earn a dollar for every black eyed pea you eat on New Year's Day. Enjoy!*

* To lower total fat by 9 grams and 80 Calories per serving, use only 3 tablespoons olive oil for the salad and 1 teaspoon canola oil and a non-stick skillet for the garlic-red pepper mixture.

New Wave Marinated 'Ahi Salad

Serves 1

*Contrasting tastes and textures—cold with warm, crisp with firm—
make this fun to eat. Each layer in this salad presents a new and wonderful flavor.
Together they are in harmony. The tortilla cup adds crunch.*

New Wave Marinade (see recipe on page 46)

2 to 3 ounces dry Japanese soba noodles or somen

Salad greens

Salad dressing of your choice

1 flour tortilla

Oil for deep-frying

3 'ahi (yellowfin tuna) fillets (2 ounces each and about 1/2-inch thick)

1 tablespoon olive oil for searing fish (or enough to coat bottom of pan)

Garnish:

Carrot, beet, and radish curls, or grated carrots and zucchini

3 cucumber slices

3 tomato wedges

Sprig of fresh cilantro

Sprinkle of black sesame seeds, chopped macadamia nuts, or chopped walnuts

Cook soba noodles (or somen) according to package directions, rinse well in cold water and drain. Take 2 to 4 tablespoons New Wave Marinade and mix it with noodles. Chill noodles in refrigerator for 20 to 30 minutes.

Marinate 'ahi fillets in mixture for 5 minutes; remove from marinade and set aside.

Deep-fry tortilla until golden brown and drain on paper towels.

Sear marinated ahi on high heat on a flat griddle or sauté pan in olive oil for about 1 minute per side. (You want the fish to remain raw in the middle.)

Place tortilla on a salad plate and arrange a handful or two of your favorite greens broken into bite-size pieces. Place the cold soba noodles on top of the greens, then arrange warm fish on top of that. Place your vegetable curls or grated vegetable garnish on top of the fish, add a sprig of cilantro, and sprinkle with black sesame seeds, or chopped nuts.

recipe continued on page 46

New Wave Marinated 'Ahi Salad
continued

Place the slices of cucumber and tomato wedges around the edge of the plate and serve with Creamy Oriental Dressing (see recipe on page 62) or your favorite dressing.

This "wok salad" offers an interesting contrast in tastes and textures between chilled greens, cold noodles, and warm fish.

You can make it a lower fat salad by omitting the deep-fried flour tortilla and using the marinade as the dressing.

New Wave Marinade

1/2 cup soy sauce

1/4 cup light salad oil

2 tablespoons mirin (Japanese sweet rice wine)

1/4 teaspoon sesame oil

1/2 tablespoon minced fresh cilantro

2 tablespoons thinly sliced green onions

1 tablespoon minced fresh garlic

1 tablespoon peeled and minced fresh ginger

1/2 teaspoon salt

1/4 teaspoon white pepper

1-1/2 teaspoons brown sugar

1/2 teaspoon ground five spice powder

1 tablespoon black sesame seeds

Pinch of dried red chili pepper flakes or 1 fresh Hawaiian chili pepper

Makes about 1 cup

Combine ingredients. Stir until sugar dissolves.

Somen Noodles with Julienne Vegetables

Serves 4

Cool noodle dishes are perfect for a hot and humid day. The julienne vegetables add crunch while the Citrus Vinaigrette puts a zing in the taste buds.

Citrus Vinaigrette (see recipe below)
1/2 pound cooked somen noodles
12 spinach leaves
1/2 cup julienned carrots
1/2 cup julienned red bell peppers
1/2 cup julienned zucchini
12 fresh basil leaves
1 tablespoon fresh minced cilantro

Cook noodles according to package directions, drain.

In a large mixing bowl, combine somen noodles with remaining ingredients. Cool. Dress with Citrus Vinaigrette.

Citrus Vinaigrette

Makes 4 cups

1 cup balsamic vinegar
1 cup fresh orange juice
2 tablespoons chopped fresh basil
2 tablespoons chopped fresh cilantro
2 tablespoons granulated sugar (or more to taste)
1 teaspoon dry mustard
Salt and pepper to taste
1 cup light salad oil

Combine all ingredients except oil. Whisk until sugar is completely dissolved and mixture is thoroughly blended. It is important to dissolve all the sugar before getting the true taste. Gradually add oil while continuing to whisk. Re-adjust seasoning with additional salt, pepper, and sugar if necessary. Keep whisking until mixed well.

* Cut the fat in this recipe by half by using only 1 cup oil while increasing both the balsamic vinegar and orange juice to 1-1/2 cups. Use agar flakes as a thickening agent and mix them prior to the addition of the oil. Remember—a little goes a long way.

GALLO *of* SONOMA
RUSSIAN RIVER VALLEY
Chardonnay
BARREL FERMENTED   *1998*

Chicken Salad Chinese-Style with "dabest" Sauce

Serves 4

The jumbo shrimp give this classic Chinese Chicken Salad a gourmet touch. Cook the shrimp just enough. If you cook them too much, they won't be tender. Black and white sesame seeds and chopped green onions give "dabest" sauce a festive look.

**"dabest" Sauce
(see recipe on page 49)**

2 pounds skinless boneless chicken thigh

**1/8 teaspoon salt
(for boiling water)**

1 pound extra jumbo shrimp (16 to 20 count), peeled and deveined

1 medium sized iceberg lettuce cut into thin strips

2 stalks of celery, cut in round slices

1 medium cucumber seeded, halved lengthwise and sliced horizontally

1 green bell pepper, julienned

1 small won bok cabbage (or Napa cabbage) sliced thinly

2 medium carrots, julienned

Garnish:

Won ton chips or fried won ton wrapper strips (see Note)

Place rinsed chicken in a pot and cover with salted water. Bring water to a simmer and boil chicken for 30 to 45 minutes. Remove chicken from pot and cool slightly. Refrigerate until completely cooled.

When chicken is cool, bring 3-inches of water to a boil in a large saucepan. Add shrimp to liquid. As soon as water returns to a boil, remove shrimp (Do not overcook).

In a large bowl, add shrimp, iceberg lettuce, celery, cucumber, green bell pepper, won bok cabbage (or Napa cabbage), carrots, and cooled chicken. Add sauce and won ton strips to salad ingredients and lightly toss. Serve immediately.

Note: *If using won ton wrappers, cut 12 pieces into thin strips. Fry in a small pot of oil heated to 375°F. Drain on paper towels and cool.*

* Why not try garnishing with baked low-fat chips to lower the fat but still keep the crunch.

"dabest" Sauce

1/4 cup granulated sugar

3/8 cup rice vinegar

2 teaspoons salt

1/2 cup salad oil

2 tablespoons white sesame seeds,
lightly toasted

1 tablespoon peeled and minced fresh
ginger

3 tablespoons chopped green onions

1 tablespoon soy sauce

1 teaspoon black sesame seeds

Makes 1-1/2 cups

Whisk together sugar, vinegar, and salt until all sugar and salt are dissolved. Gradually add salad oil while continually whisking until all oil is incorporated. Add remaining ingredients and mix well.

Chicken With Papaya and Pineapple Salad

Serves 4

The marinade works on the thinly sliced chicken giving it a zesty flavor that is mellowed by the fresh fruit. A crispy tortilla base adds a nice crunch.

1-1/2 pounds chicken breast, cut into thin strips

4 tablespoons soy sauce

4 tablespoons oyster sauce

4 teaspoons minced fresh garlic

4 teaspoons peeled and minced fresh ginger

Pinch of salt and pepper

1/4 cup salad oil

8 flour tortillas (5-inch tortillas)

Peanut oil for frying

4 handful of mixed salad greens

1 cup diced papaya

1 cup diced pineapple

Garnish:

Curls made from carrots, daikon and beets

Sam Choy's Award Winning Creamy Oriental Dressing

Marinate the chicken with soy sauce, oyster sauce, garlic, ginger, salt, and pepper about 10 minutes. Lightly spray wok with oil and heat to medium-high. Add the marinated chicken and stir-fry about 4 minutes until the chicken is just cooked. Remove from the heat.

Meanwhile in a separate large skillet, heat a small amount of oil at a time until is sizzles, fry one tortilla at a time until crisp and golden. Drain on paper towels.

Place one tortilla on a plate, top with salad greens and then a second tortilla. Continue to build the salad with cooked chicken and diced papaya and pineapple. Garnish with vegetable curls and Sam's dressing. Enjoy !

* Lower the fat by substituting Sam Choy's Creamy Oriental Dressing with Sam Choy's Reduced Fat, Reduced Calorie Creamy Oriental Dressing

Moloka'i Shrimp Spinach Salad

Serves 4

This recipe has one of just about every Island flavor. The secret is in the layering of texture and tastes. Taking the time to oven-roast the bell pepper is well worth the effort.

Shrimp Marinade (see recipe below)

Warm Spinach Salad Vinaigrette (see recipe on page 52)

I pound whole extra jumbo shrimp (16 to 20 count), peeled and deveined

4 cups fresh spinach leaves, rinsed and dried

Garnish:

I sliced oven-roasted bell pepper (see Note)

2 eggs, hard boiled and diced

I tablespoon minced macadamia nuts

Marinate shrimp for 30 minutes. Then, fry in a wok on high heat and set aside.

Pour Warm Spinach Salad Vinaigrette over spinach leaves and toss. On individual plates, layer with spinach, shrimp, eggs, bell pepper slices and macadamia nuts.

Shrimp Marinade

I cup soy sauce

2 tablespoons brown sugar

I tablespoon minced fresh garlic

2 teaspoons red chili pepper flakes

I tablespoon minced fresh cilantro

I tablespoon peeled and minced fresh ginger

1/4 teaspoon white pepper

1/2 teaspoon sesame seeds

Makes 1-1/4 cups

Combine.

Note: *To prepare bell peppers for roasting, wash and remove seeds and ribs of pepper membranes. Place cleaned peppers on a baking pan under the broiler. Char peppers under broiler until the skin blisters. Make sure to carefully turn pepper to make sure all sides blister. Place pepper in tightly sealed brown paper bag for 20 minutes, then peel off loosened skin with a knife.*

Warm Spinach Salad Vinaigrette

1/2 cup pine nuts
2 tablespoons balsamic vinegar
2 tablespoons fresh lemon juice
2 tablespoons granulated sugar
1/2 teaspoon cracked peppercorn
1/4 teaspoon sesame seeds
1/4 teaspoon red chili pepper flakes

Makes 3/4 cup

In a wok, stir vinaigrette ingredients together over medium-high heat until warm.

* Substitute 1/2 cup pine nuts with 2 tablespoons of pine nuts in 1/3 cup of julienned almonds to lower the total fat by 30 grams and 250 Calories for 3/4 cup vinaigrette.

Island-Style Seafood Salad

Serves 4

Searing marinated 'ahi, scallops and shrimp to barely medium rare is the key to this dish. Overcooking will spoil the texture and the taste.

Island-Style Seafood Marinade (see recipe below)
Seafood Salad (see recipe on page 54)
1/2 pound fresh 'ahi block (yellowfin tuna)
1/4 pound any size scallops, rinsed under cold water
1/4 pound whole extra jumbo shrimp (16 to 20 count), peeled and deveined
1/2 tablespoon vegetable oil
4 cups mixed salad greens of your choice

Rub marinade on seafood and place in a large bowl or ceramic dish. Cover and place in refrigerator for 30 minutes.

Heat oil in a wok over medium-high heat and sear fish until medium rare. Remove from wok and slice after slight cooling. Add scallops and shrimp, along with any marinade and stir-fry for about 4 minutes. Do not overcook. Cool.

Arrange a layer of greens on four large plates. Layer with shellfish and Seafood Salad and mixed greens again. Place seared fish on top of salad and serve.

Island-Style Seafood Marinade

1/2 teaspoon white pepper
I teaspoon cracked black pepper
I teaspoon minced fresh garlic
I teaspoon peeled and minced fresh ginger
I tablespoon fresh minced cilantro
I tablespoon sesame oil
I tablespoon soy sauce
Hawaiian salt to taste

Makes 1/4 cup

Combine ingredients and mix well.

Seafood Salad

Makes about 4 cups

Crabmeat and sliced Fried Fishcakes mix with seaweed and cilantro and 'inamona for a texture and flavor treat. Prepared seafood salad mix speeds up serving time while adding another layer of flavor to the mixture.

**Fried Fishcakes
(see recipe below)**

1/2 pound cooked crabmeat

1/2 cup minced onion

**1 tablespoon rinsed and
chopped ogo seaweed**

**3 tablespoons chopped
bell peppers**

**1/2 tablespoon 'inamona
(see Note)**

1/2 cup chopped green onions

**1 tablespoon chopped
fresh cilantro**

1 teaspoon red chili pepper flakes

2 teaspoon sesame oil

**1/2 pound seafood salad
(may be purchased in seafood section
of many stores)**

1 bell green peppers, sliced

In a large bowl, combine all salad ingredients and toss together.

Note: *'Inamona is a mash of roasted, salted kukui nut. Roasted salted cashew nuts can be substituted if kukui nut is unavailable*

Fried Fishcakes

Makes 1 cup sliced fishcakes

6 ounces fishcake

**2 tablespoons rinsed and chopped fresh
shiitake mushrooms**

2 tablespoons chopped green onion

Salt and pepper to taste

**1 tablespoon vegetable oil
for frying**

Mix fishcake with shiitake mushrooms, green onions, salt, and pepper. Form into thin patties. Lightly oil wok or skillet. Pan fry fishcakes over medium-high heat until slightly browned. Slice.

Cold Poached Lobster Salad

Serves 4

Often considered the "King of Seafood," just the words "Chilled Lobster" have an elegance. The combined flavors of asparagus, spinach, and a great dressing crown the king very nicely.

1 pound precooked lobster meat (see Note)
1 pound assorted mixed greens
4 fresh asparagus spears, blanched and cut into segments
1/2 cup diced carrots
1/2 cup fresh spinach leaves, cooked
1/2 cup peas, frozen or canned
1 cup mayonnaise
1/2 teaspoon white pepper
Juice of 1 lemon (about 2 tablespoons)
1/2 teaspoon salt
1/4 tablespoon curry powder
1 teaspoon minced fresh cilantro

Garnish:

Edible flowers (pansies and nasturtiums)
Cilantro sprigs

Rinse and tear (if necessary) salad greens in to bite-size pieces. Drain and refrigerate until ready to serve.

Wash asparagus and snap or trim off tough ends (generally where it breaks easily). Remove lower scales or peel bottom if desired. Cut into bite-size pieces. In a large pan, add about 1-inch of water and bring to a boil. Submerge asparagus in boiling water and simmer a few minutes and then add carrots, spinach, and peas. Simmer until slightly soft (test with a fork).

In a large bowl, combine mayonnaise, white pepper, lemon juice, salt, curry powder, and cilantro. Mix well. Fold in cooked asparagus, carrots, spinach, and peas.

On individual plates, place a handful of mixed greens and top with chilled lobster meat arranged to your liking. Add mayonnaise mixture on top of lobster meat and garnish with edible flowers and cilantro sprigs.

Note: *Frozen lobster meat now can be found in most supermarkets.*

* In place of 1 mayonnaise, use 1/3 cup mayonnaise and 2/3 cup non-fat mayonnaise to make this a guilt-free but great tasting salad.

Dungeness Crab Salad

Serves 4

This large, meaty West Coast crab takes on a real Island flavor when it is combined with ogo seaweed, fresh ginger and a toasted sesame oil dressing. The crab is available both fresh and frozen.

Crab Salad Dressing (see recipe below)

6 cups fresh salad greens

1 pound cooked crabmeat (about 2 Dungeness crabs)

1 cucumber, thinly sliced

2 green onions, thinly sliced

1 tablespoon finely chopped fresh garlic

1 red and 1 yellow bell pepper, julienned

1 tablespoon peeled and finely chopped fresh ginger

1 cup rinsed and chopped ogo seaweed

2 tablespoons granulated sugar

3 tablespoons toasted sesame seeds

3 tablespoons soy sauce

1 teaspoon garlic chili sauce

Rinse and tear (if necessary) salad greens into bite-size pieces. Drain and refrigerate until ready to serve.

Mix cooked crab meat, cucumber, green onions, garlic, bell peppers, and ginger. Toss the dressing with the crabmeat mixture. Add the remaining ingredients, tossing lightly. Chill.

Serve crab salad mixture on top of a bed of fresh salad greens.

Crab Salad Dressing

Makes 2/3 cup

Juice of 1 lemon (about 2 tablespoons)

1/4 cup rice wine vinegar

2 tablespoons toasted sesame oil

2 tablespoons peanut oil

In a separate bowl, whisk together all ingredients.

Mahimahi Lemon Pepper Salad

Serves 4

Pan fried fish tops cold somen noodles, plated over greens, drizzled with a vinegar, ginger and sugar dressing. Add a few edible flowers for color and enjoy.

4 mahimahi (dolphinfish) fillets (6 ounces each)

Lemon pepper to taste

1/2 cup all-purpose flour

Vegetable oil for frying

2 cups cooked and chilled somen noodles

1 pound mixed greens

1 cup rice wine vinegar

1 tablespoon peeled and minced fresh ginger

3 tablespoons granulated sugar

1 cup peeled and sliced cucumbers

1 cup sliced tomatoes

Garnish:

Carrot, daikon, and beet curls or julienned

Diced tofu

1 teaspoon black goma (sesame seeds)

Cilantro sprigs

Edible flowers (pansies or nasturtiums optional)

Season fish with lemon pepper seasoning and dredge in flour. Pan fry on medium-high heat until nicely brown. Set aside.

Cook somen noodles according to package directions. Drain and set aside.

Rinse mixed greens and drain. Set aside.

In a small bowl, mix vinegar, ginger, and sugar until sugar dissolves.

Place greens on individual salad plates. Top with somen noodles, cucumbers, and tomatoes. Place mahimahi on top of salad. Drizzle dressing over entire salad.

Garnish with vegetable curls, tofu, black sesame seeds, fresh cilantro sprigs, and edible flowers.

* Sparingly prepare a non-stick pan with vegetable oil spray to lower the fat.

Lasagna-Style Hibachi Tofu Salad

Serves 2

*Stacking the tofu gives this salad a unique look.
The hibachi grill gives it a unique flavor; the Creamy Oriental Dressing
and Ginger Pesto make the flavor double-good.*

**Lasagna-Style Hibachi Tofu Salad
Marinade (see recipe on page 60)**

**Creamy Oriental Dressing and Wasabi
Vinaigrette (see recipes on page 62)**

20 ounces firm tofu

4 tablespoons olive oil

1/2 cup julienned zucchini

1/2 cup julienned sweet onions

1/2 cup julienned carrots

1/2 cup julienned red bell peppers

1/2 cup julienned yellow bell peppers

1/2 cup bean sprouts

1/2 cup sliced shiitake mushrooms

Salt and pepper to taste

**1 to 2 handfuls rinsed spring mixed
greens**

Garnish:

Ginger Pesto (see recipe on page 60)

Drain tofu and slice the whole block lengthwise into 4 equal sections. Marinate for 1 to 2 hours.

Prepare coals in hibachi.

In wok or sauté pan, heat olive oil until very hot, but not smoking. Add julienned vegetables, bean sprouts, and mushrooms. Stir-fry for 2 to 3 minutes or until vegetables are just wilted. Season with salt and pepper.

Add a handful or two of spring mixed greens and remove quickly from wok.

Remove tofu from marinade, cook on hibachi over hot coals (2 to 3 minutes on each side), then remove from heat.

To serve, place a small amount of stir-fried vegetables on salad plate, place 1 slice of tofu on top of vegetables, put a layer of vegetables on tofu, and continue alternating tofu and vegetables until you finish with a layer of vegetables on top. Garnish with Ginger Pesto and drizzle dressing over each layer, either Creamy Oriental or Wasabi Vinaigrette, or both.

Lasagna-Style Hibachi Tofu Salad Marinade

Makes 2 cups

2 cloves garlic, minced
1-1/2 cups soy sauce
1 cup granulated sugar
1/4 cup peeled and minced fresh ginger
2 tablespoons thinly sliced green onions
1 tablespoon fresh cilantro
1 teaspoon sesame oil
1/8 teaspoon white pepper

Combine ingredients and mix until sugar is dissolved.

Ginger Pesto

Makes about 1-3/4 cups

1/4 cup peeled and minced fresh ginger
1/2 cup chopped green onions
8 fresh peeled garlic cloves (about 1 ounce)
1/4 cup fresh cilantro
1 cup salad oil (like canola oil)
Salt and pepper to taste

Combine ginger, green onions, garlic, cilantro and salt and pepper in a food processor and puree for 15 seconds. With the processor running, pour salad oil slowly through the feeding tube in a steady stream. When well blended, this can be used immediately or refrigerated for later use.

Spicy Squid Salad

Serves 8

*Catching squid is half the fun. If you can't go squidding,
buy fresh from the local fish market, already cleaned. This one is only blanched,
then chilled and served in icy-cold bowls. Add the Hawaiian chili peppers
just to taste, not to curl your hair.*

4 quarts water

2 tablespoons salt

2 pounds squid (already cleaned)

2 large tomatoes, diced

3/4 cup diced red onion

**3 tablespoons diced
Hawaiian chili peppers**

1/2 cup chopped fresh cilantro

1 teaspoon minced fresh garlic

3/4 cup olive oil

1/4 cup rice wine vinegar

1/4 cup fresh lime juice

Chill serving bowls in the freezer.

Bring four quarts of water and salt to boil in a large pan.

Slice squid into 1/4 to 1/3 inch rings. Add squid to boiling water and blanch 30 seconds. Drain squid in a colander and immediately rinse under cold running water. Shake to remove excess water and place squid in a large glass or stainless steel bowl.

Add remaining ingredients and toss to combine. Cover with plastic wrap and chill until ready to serve. This dish is best served in chilled bowls.

* Replace olive oil in this recipe with less extra virgin olive oil. The flavor is fuller so you can use less without losing taste.

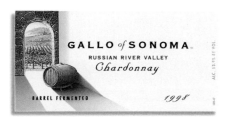

Sam's Signature
Salad Dressings

*The thing about these dressings is that they are good enough
to just eat with a spoon. Each one has a "best use," but that shouldn't stop you
from trying them on whatever strikes your fancy. They work with salad,
seafood, pasta and even as sandwich spreads and dips.*

Creamy Oriental

3 cups mayonnaise
1/2 cup soy sauce
3/4 cup granulated sugar
1/4 teaspoon white pepper
1-1/2 tablespoons black sesame seeds
1 tablespoon sesame oil

Makes 4 cups

Whisk all of the ingredients together until
well blended. If the consistency is too thick,
whisk in a few drops of water at a time, until
you get the consistency you desire.

Wasabi Vinaigrette

2 cups freshly squeezed orange juice
2 tablespoons sesame seeds
3 tablespoons granulated sugar
1/2 cup canola oil
3 tablespoons vinegar
2 tablespoons soy sauce
Salt to taste
2 tablespoons wasabi powder

Makes 3 cups

Combine ingredients and mix together until
well blended.

**Certain salads need spicing up to reach their
peak. Wasabi adds a whole different flavor. I
knew it was real popular with sushi and sashimi.
So I wanted to play with it in a vinaigrette where
people would notice it and have it wake up their
taste buds, but where it wouldn't be
overpowering.*

Sam's Special Thousand Island

2 cups mayonnaise

1/2 cup half and half

4 teaspoons drained sweet pickle relish

4 tablespoons chili sauce

1/2 tablespoon black sesame seeds

1/2 teaspoon dried red chili pepper flakes

White pepper to taste

2 hard cooked eggs, chopped

1/2 cup diced tofu

Makes 3-1/2 cups

Combine mayonnaise, half and half, pickle relish, chili sauce, sesame seeds, and chili flakes; mix well. Gently fold in tofu and chopped eggs.

Thousand Island dressing is very basic and easy to make. To make it unique, tofu and hard-boiled eggs are added to give the dressing a texture, almost as if the dressing is a salad in itself. This dressing can turn a simple salad into something very special.

Garlic Ranch Dressing

3 cloves garlic, minced

1/2 cup minced onions

1/4 cup granulated sugar

1/4 cup red wine vinegar

1/2 cup olive oil

2 cups mayonnaise

Salt and pepper to taste

2 teaspoons dry mustard

1 tablespoon minced fresh oregano

1 tablespoon chopped fresh basil

Makes 4 cups

Combine all ingredients and whisk until thoroughly blended. Chill.

This dressing is creamy and rich and makes eating salads a very memorable experience. I love to use garlic in my cooking because it spices up and brings out the flavor of whatever you put it on. Ranch dressing is very versatile. It can be used for salads, sandwiches, and dips as well.

Sweet and Sour Cucumber Vinaigrette

1 cup white vinegar

1/2 cup water

3/4 cup granulated sugar

1 cup very thinly sliced cucumbers,

1/2 tablespoon peeled and grated fresh ginger

Pinch of salt

White pepper to taste

Makes about 3 cups

Combine all ingredients and blend until sugar dissolves. Chill.

* *This vinaigrette was inspired by a simple Asian dipping sauce. By adding a few more ingredients, this vinaigrette goes well on salad, crispy won ton or spring rolls and with spicy lamb or poached fish.*

Island French

I teaspoon lime juice

I cup ketchup

I cup cider vinegar

3/4 cup granulated sugar

White pepper and salt to taste

I teaspoon dry mustard

1/2 medium-size Maui onion, finely minced

I clove garlic, minced

1/4 cup light salad oil

Makes 4 cups

In a blender, combine all ingredients, except for the oil. Purée for about 1 minute; then begin adding oil slowly. Purée for about 2 more minutes or until all of the oil has been added. Re-adjust seasonings if necessary. Total blending time will be 3 to 4 minutes. Refrigerate.

*This is a very classic, yet "local-style" dressing. I think you'll enjoy it.

Big "O" Surprise

I can (12-ounce) V-8 vegetable juice cocktail

I teaspoon minced onion

I clove garlic, minced

I teaspoon chopped parsley

I teaspoon chopped fresh cilantro

1/2 cup thinly sliced green onions

I tablespoon vinegar

I tablespoon lime juice

I tablespoon each minced red and yellow bell pepper

Makes 2 cups

Combine all ingredients and mix well. Chill.

* You'll be surprised how good this tastes.

Side dishes aren't step-children. They are the real thing. The real accompaniment to an entrée. This is the place in your menu where you can throw in a surprise. Say you are doing a beef dish. Surprise the taste buds with a sauté of fennel, shiitake mushrooms and pumpkin.

The selection you make for side dishes can add the wonderful ethnic food mix for which Hawai'i is famous. Serve pickled, steamed, and stir-fried vegetables with Asian flavors. Make a dressing of Portuguese sweet bread. Try Japanese tempura, add Chinese-style sausage to potatoes, or the wonderful taste of fermented black beans to almost any vegetable.

I like to mix and match. The family knows to expect the unexpected with my side dishes. Sides are the place to start the kids cooking. My dad started me with cleaning the vegetables. Then he showed me how to use a knife, how to get the slices of pepper or onion to be the same size. I was allowed to nibble between tasks. Carrots were like candy to me. When I ran out of veggies to chop, I practiced on ti leaves and the backyard hedge. And I drove him crazy. I asked a million questions. When I mastered a new skill, he smiled. That's what we need to do with kids. We need to teach them, give them a task and praise them when they get it right.

Remember to taste while you cook. On the show I'm always taking a taste here and there. That's how I know if there is enough garlic! When you are preparing a side dish, keep your entrée in mind. Imagine how the two flavors will complement one another. Side dishes can be signature dishes. Take my Garlic Mashed Potatoes and their cousin, Kahuku Corn Smashed Potatoes. Mention that dish and everyone knows it's Sam's sides! Hey, have some fun here!

Carrots and Cranberries

Serves 6

This looks and smells like the holidays. As a side dish, this is perfect any time fresh cranberries are available. Serve with poultry, pork or even lamb.

1 cup fresh cranberries
2 apples
4 cups fresh grated carrots
1/4 cup brown sugar
1/2 cup apple cider
1/4 cup butter

Preheat the oven to 350°F.

Wash the cranberries. Grate the apples and mix the apples and cranberries with all the remaining ingredients, except the butter. Place the ingredients in a buttered casserole and dot with remaining butter. Cover and bake for 40 minutes. Stir once during baking.

Sauté of Fennel, Shiitake Mushrooms and Pumpkin

Serves 4 to 6

Fennel is that celery-looking plant that tastes like licorice. It blends really well with the flavors of the mushrooms, a little pork, a good amount of garlic, and the pumpkin.

3 cups cubed pork

2 tablespoons minced fresh garlic

Salt and pepper to taste

I tablespoon soy sauce

2 cups thinly sliced pumpkin

I cup chicken stock or low-sodium chicken broth

I large fennel bulb, sliced

I cup rinsed and sliced fresh shiitake mushrooms

I cup julienned carrots

I bell pepper seeded and sliced (any color)

In a large wok, brown pork over medium heat. Add minced garlic and salt and pepper to taste. Stir until garlic is browned. Then add soy sauce, pumpkin, chicken stock, sliced fennel, and shiitake mushrooms. Simmer until vegetables are cooked, stirring occasionally. Add remaining ingredients and simmer until tender.

* For the least amount of fat in this great tasting dish, use a lean pork loin with all visible fat trimmed.

Jamaican Roasted Pumpkin

Serves 4

*This dark golden pumpkin, seasoned with sugar and pepper,
makes a perfect side dish for nearly any meal. Be sure to watch your oven
when you roast in very hot oil.*

3/4 cup olive oil

**1 red-fleshed pumpkin
(about 3-1/4 pounds)**

2 tablespoons light brown sugar

1 teaspoon ground cinnamon

Salt to taste

**Freshly ground black pepper
to taste**

Preheat oven to 550°F.

Put the olive oil in a roasting pan, place pan in the oven, and heat until the oil smokes (but does not catch fire!)

Cut pumpkin into 3-inch chunks and put them carefully into the hot olive oil.

Blend the sugar, cinnamon and a pinch of salt. When the pumpkin begins to brown, remove the pan from the oven and sprinkle the pumpkin with the sugar mixture. Stir well to coat all surfaces with a wooden spoon.

Return the roasting pan to the oven and bake until the pumpkin is a rich caramel color, about 40 minutes.

Drain the pumpkin in a colander to remove excess oil. Sprinkle with freshly ground black pepper and enjoy!

GALLO *of* SONOMA
RUSSIAN RIVER VALLEY
Pinot Noir
BARREL AGED   *1998*

Harvard Beets

*These two side dishes are favorites with main courses
of chicken or beef. The garlic mashed potatoes are unforgettable!*

2 cans (15-ounces each) sliced beets
(reserve liquid)
2 tablespoons granulated sugar (see Note)
I tablespoon vinegar (see Note)
2 tablespoons cornstarch mixed with
1-1/2 tablespoons water
Dash of white pepper

Combine sugar, beet liquid, and vinegar in a saucepan and heat to a boil. Gradually add cornstarch mixture, cooking and stirring until you get the consistency you like. For a thicker sauce, add more cornstarch paste .

Note: *Because beets come packed in various amounts of liquid, you may need to adjust the amount of sugar and vinegar until you get just the right balanced taste of sweet and sour.*

Add a dash of white pepper, fold in the beets, and heat thoroughly.

Garlic Mashed Potatoes

Makes about 6 cups

2-1/4 pounds potatoes
4 whole cloves garlic
1/2 pound butter
6 tablespoons heavy cream
Salt and white pepper to taste

Fill a pot with 3-inches of cold water. Peel and cut the potatoes into 1-inch cubes and add them to the pot. Add additional cold water to cover potatoes. Add garlic and bring to a boil. Cook for 8 to 10 minutes or until done. Drain.

Purée in a food processor, or whip with an electric mixer. Add the butter and cream. Season with salt and white pepper. Serve immediately.

Chicken Long Rice

Serves 12

*This is an acquired taste. Kids joke that it looks like worms.
Once you savor the dish with the chicken and shredded vegetables, accompanied by
some fresh poi, green onions and Hawaiian salt, you will never pass it by again,
no matter what the kids say!*

4 ounces long rice
20 dried shiitake mushrooms
4 cups chicken broth
**2 pounds skinless boneless chicken,
cubed**
2-inch finger of fresh ginger, crushed
1 medium onion, minced
2 cups thinly sliced celery
2 carrots, julienned
6 green onions, cut in 1-inch lengths

Soak long rice in warm water for 1 hour. Soak mushrooms in warm water for 20 minutes and drain. Remove stems and slice caps.

Pour chicken broth into a large pot, add chicken and ginger, and simmer for 5 minutes. Add onion, celery, carrots, and mushrooms, and simmer another 4 to 5 minutes.

Drain long rice and cut into 3-inch lengths. Add long rice and green onions to the pot and stir. Cook an additional 5 minutes or until long rice becomes translucent.

Orange Glazed Sweet Potatoes

Serves 8

Sweet potatoes, boiled, steamed, baked, we like them every way.
Baked with some fresh-made marmalade they are a really fine side dish.
The secret is the orange juice for moistness.

6 sweet potatoes, boiled with the skin on

I cup orange marmalade

I cup Pineapple/Papaya Marmalade (see recipe below)

1/2 cup orange juice

I tablespoon butter

Additional butter to taste

Salt to taste

Preheat oven to 325°F.

In a large pot, boil or steam sweet potatoes until 3/4 cooked. Peel sweet potatoes and cut into thick slices. Add marmalades and orange juice and toss to cover potatoes. Butter a casserole and layer potatoes, sprinkle lightly with salt and dot with butter. Bake for 30 to 40 minutes or until browned and candied.

* To prepare the casserole, lightly spray with a butter-flavored vegetable oil spray in place of butter.

Pineapple/Papaya Marmalade

Makes about 6 to 8 cups

I pineapple, peeled and diced small (4 cups)

4 medium papayas, seeded and diced (6 cups)

I cup granulated sugar

Place pineapple, papayas, and sugar in a sauce pot and cook over medium-low heat until fruit is softened and incorporated with sugar thoroughly, about 30 to 45 minutes. Cool.

Lup Cheung Lyonnaise Potatoes

Serves 4

Lup Cheung Chinese-style sausage, sliced thin and cooked with the onions flavors the potatoes and adds the oil to turn them a delicious golden brown.

3 ounces lup cheung, thinly sliced

1 round onion, sliced

2 teaspoons minced fresh garlic

2 russet potatoes, rinsed, sliced and blanched

1 tablespoon butter

Heat a wok or heavy skillet to medium. Put in lup cheung, onions and garlic. Stir constantly to prevent garlic from burning. When onion is translucent, add sliced potatoes and butter; stir. This dish is ready to serve when the potatoes are cooked.

Sweet Potato Coconut Casserole

Serves 6

If you want to start a new holiday tradition, serve this fresh coconut and macadamia nut version of the classic sweet potato dish. Your family may never want that old marshmallow topped version again.

4 cups sweet potatoes steamed until soft and mashed

1/3 cup brown sugar

1/3 cup butter

1/2 cup coconut milk

1/2 cup milk

1/3 cup fresh coconut, grated

1/3 cup toasted and chopped macadamia nuts

2 tablespoons butter, melted

Preheat oven to 325°F.

Whisk potatoes, sugar, butter. milk, and coconut milk until light and fluffy. Prepare 2-quart casserole with vegetable oil spray. Pour potato mixture into casserole.

Mix coconut, macadamia nuts, brown sugar, and melted butter. Sprinkle coconut mixture on top of the sweet potatoes. Bake for 1 hour or until potatoes are heated through and the top is crunchy.

* You can lower the fat in this dish by substituting one or more of the following: replace some or all of the butter with buttermilk; substitute low-fat coconut milk for the coconut milk; and use toasted chopped almonds in place of the macadamia nuts.

Wok-Fried Red Lettuce and Red Oak
with Ginger Slivers and Garlic

Serves 4

*Make that wok smoke again, then toss in the lettuce
so quickly that it almost doesn't hit the pan. Add a few dried seaweed flakes
for an Island taste and it's ready to serve.*

I tablespoon light salad oil

I head red leaf lettuce, rinsed and leaves separated

I head red oak lettuce, rinsed and leaves separated

I tablespoon peeled and finely slivered fresh ginger

I tablespoon minced fresh garlic

I teaspoon Hawaiian salt

1/4 cup chicken stock or low-sodium chicken broth

I tablespoon furikake (dried seaweed flakes blended with sesame seeds and seasoning)

I tablespoon black sesame seeds

I tablespoon chopped green onions

Heat oil in wok until smoking. Add lettuce, ginger, garlic, salt, and then chicken stock. Cook about 1 minute until lettuce is wilted. Place in a bowl, then sprinkle with furikake, sesame seeds and green onions.

Chinese Pasta Primavera

Serves 8

*Pasta is trendy and classic . It can seem very Asian
and very Italian at the same time. The more sautéed vegetables you toss in a bowl of
fresh-cooked pasta, the more the mouth waters. Add snow peas and Thai basil
and you are in Asia. Add a bit of Parmesan and you can be in Italy, too.*

1 pound dry linguine

1 medium red bell pepper, cut into strips

1 medium yellow bell pepper, cut into strips

2 medium zucchini, trimmed but not peeled, sliced

1/2 pound broccoli florets

1/2 pound fresh asparagus, cut in 1-inch pieces

1/2 pound whole sugar snap peas or Chinese snow peas

6 shallots or green onions, sliced very thin

1 clove garlic, minced

1 tablespoon butter

1 tablespoon olive oil

1/4 cup chopped fresh cilantro

2 tablespoons chopped fresh Thai basil

Salt and pepper to taste

1 tablespoon soy sauce

1/4 cup freshly grated Parmesan cheese

Fill a large pot with water and begin heating it for the pasta.

In a large skillet or wok, heat oil and butter and stir-fry vegetables, onion, and garlic about 3 minutes. Add cilantro and basil and cook another minute, or until vegetables are done to your taste (they should be a little crunchy). Season vegetables with salt and pepper and mix with soy sauce

When the water boils, add linguine and cook al dente according to package directions. Drain. Toss vegetables with pasta and sprinkle with Parmesan cheese.

Hibachi Mixed Vegetables

Serves 4

The variety of colors in this side dish makes it pretty for the plate. The secret here is the 30-minute multi-spiced marinade. Once these tasty vegetables come off the hibachi they won't be on that plate long.

Mixed Vegetable Marinade (see recipe below)
2 cups oval sliced zucchini
2 cups oval sliced yellow squash
I cup sliced red bell pepper
8 fresh rinsed and quartered fresh shiitake mushrooms

Mix sliced vegetables with marinade for 30 minutes.

Prepare coals in a hibachi (or barbecue grill). Cook vegetables over hibachi until done.

Mixed Vegetable Marinade

I teaspoon chopped fresh garlic
1/4 teaspoon black pepper
1/4 teaspoon chili sauce
I teaspoon chopped fresh cilantro
I teaspoon thyme leaves
I tablespoon white wine
I tablespoon salad oil
I teaspoon sesame oil
1/4 teaspoon soy sauce
1/4 teaspoon oyster sauce

Makes 1/3 Cup

Mix all ingredients together.

For a time beef was getting a "bad rap" in the food marketplace. Like anything else, we need to think moderation. It isn't so much watching what you eat but rather how much you eat of any one thing. When they tell you to cut your calories in half that means eat only half the cream pie! Just kidding.

Seriously, most of us enjoy a really good cut of prime rib or a hamburger so juicy it runs off your chin. Beef has great taste. But, like many other foods, we simply need to adjust the portion size. Beef is easy to prepare. What I like to do is the simple dish that lets the beef flavor through. Something like a stir-fry pepper beef with julienned vegetables, or Kalbi ribs on the hibachi. I like beef recipes with an attitude, dishes that really make your taste buds take notice. Like Fiery Chinese Beef full of ginger, garlic, hot sauce and black beans. All my TV beef recipes have one thing in common, they will always be successful if you follow the easy steps.

One of the nice things about living in Hawai'i is that you can cook outdoors nearly any day. Of course, if the aroma of your neighbors' barbecue comes wafting your way, you can bet you'll be firing up the hibachi real soon. It is irresistible! And, there is something about cooking outdoors. Maybe it's back to a simple life, or "small kid days." Maybe it is just that primitive feeling of cooking over the fire. Whatever it is, it is worth taking the time. And it is worth showing the kids how to do it, well and safely.

Stir-Fry Pepper Beef

Serves 4

Dashi is a clear Japanese Fish broth, found in stores as instant granules or tea bags. Add a bit of oyster sauce and you've got great flavor. Bell peppers are best when they are still crisp.

2 tablespoons salad oil

I pound beef cut into strips

2 small onions, julienned

2 stalks celery, julienned

2 small green bell peppers, cut into 1/2-inch strips

2 small red bell peppers, cut into 1/2-inch strips

2 tablespoons minced fresh garlic

2 tablespoons peeled and minced fresh ginger

Pinch of salt and pepper

1/2 cup prepared dashi (tuna flake broth) or low-sodium chicken broth

2 tablespoons soy sauce

2 tablespoons oyster sauce

4 cups soft noodles or rice

2 tablespoons cornstarch in 2 tablespoons water for thickening

Heat 1 tablespoon salad oil in wok until just smoking. Add beef, onions, and celery, cook about 1 minute. Add bell peppers, minced garlic, ginger, salt, pepper, dashi, soy sauce, and oyster sauce and cook about 3 minutes more, being careful not to overcook the meat. Add cornstarch mixture to thicken. Pour over noodles or rice.

GALLO SONOMA
SONOMA COUNTY
Cabernet Sauvignon

The Best Beef Stew

Serves 6

*The natural flavors of the vegetables and the beef
really shine through on this classic dish. The surprise combo of beef stock and
chicken stock give the gravy a smooth, long simmering taste.*

4 pounds chuck roast

Salt and pepper to taste

**All-purpose flour to dust meat (about
1 cup)**

1/2 cup salad oil

2 cloves garlic, crushed

1 small onion, minced

1/2 cup chopped celery leaves

5 cups beef stock or low-sodium broth

2 cups chicken broth

1-1/2 cups tomato paste

3 medium carrots, stew-cut

4 potatoes, stew-cut

2 medium onions, stew-cut

4 stalks celery, stew-cut

**Mochiko (sweet rice flour) and water
to thicken**

Cut beef into bite-size pieces and sprinkle with salt and pepper. Dust beef with flour.

In a large pot, heat oil over a medium heat and brown meat with garlic, onion, and celery leaves for about 10 minutes or until well browned. Keep stirring to avoid burning.

Drain oil and add beef and chicken broth and tomato paste. Stir and bring mixture to a boil, then reduce to simmer. Cover and let cook about 1 hour, or until beef is tender.

Add carrots and potatoes and cook 5 minutes. Add onion chunks and celery and cook 10 minutes more. Adjust seasonings with salt and pepper.

Mix mochiko and water into a thick syrup. Bring stew to a boil and add mochiko mixture a little at a time, simmering and stirring until you get the right consistency. Remove from heat and refrigerate overnight. Flavors in this stew are best if given a chance to blend.

Papa Choy's Beef Tomato

Serves 6

*Watching papa Choy chopping vegetables at the speed of light,
then stir-frying them with paper-thin slices of beef was a treat to the eyes
as well as the taste buds. Even the marinade and the sauce take
only minutes to combine. Make sure the rice pot is done.*

**Papa Choy's Beef Marinade
(see recipe below)**

**Papa Choy's Sauce
(see recipe on page 88)**

1 pound round or flank steak

1 tablespoon oil

**3 medium fresh tomatoes, cut into
wedges**

1 medium onion, sliced into half moons

1 large green pepper, sliced into strips

**4 stalks green onions, cut into
1-inch lengths**

**2 stalks celery, thinly sliced on the
diagonal**

salt and pepper to taste

Slice beef thinly into strips, or bite-size pieces. Massage Papa Choy's Beef Marinade into meat. Let marinate for 30 minutes.

Heat 1 tablespoon oil in a wok or frying pan on medium-high. Stir-fry beef about 2 minutes and remove from pan; set aside. Add vegetables to pan and stir-fry until onions are translucent, about 3 minutes. Add Papa Choy's Sauce to vegetables and cook about 2 minutes or until it comes to a boil. Add beef and adjust seasonings with salt and pepper. Serve over hot rice.

Papa Choy's Beef Marinade

Makes 1/4 cup

1 tablespoon soy sauce

1 tablespoon sherry

1 tablespoon oil

1-1/2 teaspoons granulated sugar

1 clove garlic, minced

1/4 finger fresh ginger, sliced

Mix all ingredients together.

Papa Choy's Sauce

1 cup chicken broth
1 tablespoon cornstarch
2 tablespoons soy sauce
2 teaspoons salt
2 teaspoons brown sugar
1 teaspoon oyster sauce

Makes 1-1/4 cups

Combine sauce ingredients, mix well, and set aside.

Beef Sukiyaki

Serves 6

This dish is picture-perfect when you serve it from the wok. It is like a painting in food. Take time to shop for the konnyaku and both rice wines. The flavor results are worth it.

Sukiyaki Sauce (see recipe below)

2 pounds sirloin beef, cut into bite-sized pieces

1/2 red bell pepper, julienned

1/2 pound sliced konnyaku (Asian gel-like cake made from yam-like tuber)

1 carrot, julienned

1/2 Maui onion, sliced

1/2 cup watercress cut into 1 inch pieces

1 cup firm tofu, cubed

8 fresh rinsed and halved fresh shiitake mushrooms

Peeled and grated fresh ginger to taste

1/4 cup green onions, sliced into 1/2 inch segments

In a large wok, stir-fry the beef halfway and add the sauce. While simmering the meat in the sauce, add the red bell peppers and konnyaku first. Keep everything separate in the wok as it makes for a nice arrangement. Simmer the peppers and konnyaku for about a minute, then add the carrots and onions, followed by the watercress, tofu, and shiitake mushrooms following the same procedure as mentioned earlier. Simmer for a minute or so until all vegetables are tender. Sprinkle with green onion segments and serve from the wok!

* To achieve the same taste, but lower both fat and Calories, use a round tip beef instead of sirloin and substitute the firm tofu with extra firm low-fat tofu.

Sukiyaki Sauce

Makes 2 cups

1 cup dark soy sauce

1 cup mirin (Japanese sweet rice wine)

1/2 cup water

7 tablespoons granulated sugar

1/4 cup sake (sweet Japanese rice wine)

2 teaspoons peeled and grated fresh ginger

Combine ingredients and mix well until sugar is dissolved.

Fiery Chinese Beef

Serves 4

*Have the plates ready because this meal is really quick to fix.
We use the quick-cooking rice and the meat cooks for only two minutes,
then the hot sauce and seasonings jump in. A cold bottle of
Sam's beer adds a perfect balance.*

**1 can (15 ounce) oriental broth
or low-sodium chicken broth**

1-1/4 cups water

**2-1/2 cups uncooked
5-minute rice**

2 teaspoons peanut oil

**1 pound sirloin, cut into
thin 2 inch strips**

1 pound frozen mixed vegetables

2 teaspoons minced fresh garlic

**1 teaspoon peeled and minced
fresh ginger**

1 teaspoon granulated sugar

1 teaspoon black bean sauce

1/2 teaspoon hot sauce

2 tablespoons cornstarch

In a 2-quart pot combine rice with 1 cup broth and 1-1/4 cups water. Bring to a boil, reduce heat and simmer until done.

Heat peanut oil in sauté pan and add meat and stir-fry beef for approximately 2 minutes. Add vegetables, garlic, sugar, ginger, black bean sauce, and hot sauce. Mix well. Simmer for 3 minutes.

Mix cornstarch with remaining broth into a paste. Add cornstarch-broth mixture to thicken sauce. Let simmer 1 minute.

Serve over rice.

* If beef is cut into thin strips, then substituting sirloin with a lean round tip cut will lower the fat and Calories without decreasing the flavor.

GALLO *of* SONOMA
DRY CREEK VALLEY
Zinfandel

BARREL AGED   *1997*

Roasted Sausages and Peppers

Serves 4

This open face hoagie is ready fast. One of the best parts—
the variety of mustards you serve. To make the mustards even better, make them
"beer mustard" by stirring a bit of Sam's brew into each one.

4 hoagie rolls (6-inch loaf French
or Italian bread)
2 pounds assorted sausages,
cut on diagonal
4 bell peppers (yellow, red,
orange, green), julienned
I/2 cup julienned red onions
I/2 cup julienned Maui or
globe onions
I teaspoon salt
I teaspoon pepper

Assorted mustards
and sauces:

Dijon, whole grain,
deli, plain yellow, beer,
hot sauce, horseradish

Optional condiments:

sauerkraut or pepperoncini
(2- to 3-inch long bright red chilies)

In a large pan, fry sausages over medium-high heat. Sauté peppers and onions until peppers are limp and onions are translucent. Season with salt and pepper. Set aside.

Slice hoagie rolls in half. Spread mustard of your choice on each half of the roll. Then build the hoagie by layering sausage slices, bell peppers, and onions on top of hoagie roll. Drizzle mustards and optional condiments and serve with sauerkraut or pepperoncini chilies if desired.

Hawaiian Pulehu Tri-Tip Steak

Serves 4 to 6

*Crusty on the outside and rare on the inside. That's the secret
to this mouth-watering dish. It could almost be called beef sashimi.
Hot is wonderful, but cold sandwiches the next day allow
the flavors to mature very nicely, thank you.*

**2-1/2 pounds tri-tip steak (triangular
tip of the sirloin)**
1/2 cup sea salt
1 tablespoon minced fresh garlic
1/2 tablespoon cracked peppercorns
1 tablespoon granulated sugar

Prepare your charcoal for grilling.

Rub salt, garlic, pepper, and sugar into
the meat and let sit 30 minutes. Pulehu
in Hawaiian means "to broil on hot
embers" and that's what you do, turning
the meat every 4 minutes until done.
Total cooking time is about 10 to 15
minutes, depending on the thickness of
the cut.

Tip: *This is a big piece of beef and the
crusty outside and rare inside makes it
almost like beef sashimi. It's great eating
when it's hot, and it makes the best cold
sandwiches the next day after the flavors
have had a chance to be absorbed all
through the meat.*

Kalbi Ribs

Serves 4

*Try these if you want something even better than
your neighborhood Korean barbecue. Make your own marinade with just enough
garlic and plenty of black pepper. Grill on a hibachi for the very best flavor.
Keep chili pepper water on hand to spice up a variety of dishes.*

**Kalbi Ribs Marinade
(see recipe below)**

**12 pieces Beef Short Ribs
(1/2" cut)**

Vegetable oil cooking spray

Marinate beef short ribs for 1 hour in the
refrigerator. Coat grill rack with vegetable oil
cooking spray. Grill ribs over medium-hot
coals for 5 minutes per side or until done.

** To lower fat, buy lean ribs with visible fat
trimmed and use the lower-fat version of the
Kalbi Rib Marinade.*

Kalbi Ribs Marinade

Makes about 1 cup

2 tablespoons chopped garlic

**2 teaspoons Chili Pepper Water
(see recipe below)**

2 teaspoons black pepper

1/2 cup white wine

1/2 cup salad oil

Whisk ingredients together.

** Decrease the salad oil to 1/4 cup. There is still
plenty of marinade with half the fat.*

Chili Pepper Water

Makes 1-1/4 cups

2 Hawaiian chili peppers, minced

1 cup water

1/4 cup vinegar

1 teaspoon Hawaiian salt

1/4 teaspoon fresh garlic, crushed

Combine ingredients in a small sauce pan.
Bring water to a simmer and cook for 15
minutes. Set aside.

Prime Rib Roast

Serves 6 to 8

*This is an easy dish. But, if you've never done it before,
it can be real challenging. Make sure you have a pan large enough.
Pre-heat that oven to 450 to 500°F. The secret is to sear the outside of the meat,
then turn it down, add the stock and let it cook to medium rare.*

5 pounds prime rib roast
1/4 cup sea salt or Hawaiian salt
1/4 cup cracked peppercorn
Salt and pepper to taste
1/4 cup chopped fresh garlic
1/4 cup chopped fresh rosemary
2 cups beef stock
Au Jus (see recipe below)

Preheat oven to 450°F. Massage in sea salt and cracked peppercorn into prime rib. Add more salt and pepper to taste. Add chopped garlic and rosemary to prime rib and place into a baking pan.

Sear in oven for 30 minutes. Add beef stock and turn oven down to 325°F. (See Au Jus directions). Roast for 2 to 2-1/2 hours. Using an internal meat thermometer, insert thermometer into center of roast. Meat will be medium-rare at 140°F, medium at 160°F; and well-done at 170°F. When roast is at the desired stage, take roast out of oven and let stand for half an hour before cutting to prevent loss of juices.

Au Jus

Makes about 3 cups

2 onions, large dice
1 carrot, large dice
2 stalks celery, large dice
8 cloves garlic, peeled
2 cups beef stock

Once the oven is turned down, add chopped onion, celery, carrots, and garlic cloves into roasting pan. When roast is done, strain out drippings and add a little more beef stock if needed.

GALLO *of* SONOMA
SONOMA COUNTY
Cabernet Sauvignon

BARREL AGED   *1997*

Stir-Fried Beef with Honaunau Snow Peas

Serves 4

Cleaning the snow peas takes a few minutes, but the job is well worth the result. Watch carefully, don't overcook the peas. The beef should be fork-tender. Remember to put the rice pot on before you cook the peas and beef. Before you know it, the dish is done.

1 pound lean beef

2 tablespoons cornstarch

2 teaspoons granulated sugar

1 tablespoon soy sauce

1-1/2 tablespoons sweet vermouth

1-1/2 tablespoons water

3 tablespoons oil

1/2 finger of peeled and julienned fresh ginger

1/2 pound snow peas, ends removed

1 cup chicken broth

Salt and pepper to taste

1 tablespoon water

Slice beef thinly, against the grain. In a shallow bowl, mix 1 tablespoon cornstarch, 1 teaspoon sugar, soy sauce, and vermouth. Massage into meat for 2 to 3 minutes. Let beef marinate for 2 or 3 minutes.

Meanwhile, heat 1 tablespoon oil on medium-high heat in wok or sauté pan. Stir-fry ginger a minute or two. Add snow peas and stir-fry 1 or 2 minutes more. Remove ginger and snow peas and set aside.

Add 2 tablespoons oil and stir-fry beef on medium-high heat until beef begins to brown. Add broth, snow peas, and ginger and bring to a boil. Season with salt and pepper to taste. Combine cornstarch, sugar, and water to make a thickening paste. Return broth to a boil and add paste while stirring until broth is thickened. Serve with hot rice.

* The hardest part of this dish is cutting the beef and cleaning the snow peas. It's quick and really delicious. Remember, don't overcook the snow peas.

Yankee Pot Roast

Serves 8 to 10

In a slow cooker or in a large pot, this is one of the easiest dinners ever cooked. After you brown the meat, you boil the broth and add an assortment of vegetables. Add some lovely bay leaf and rosemary and put on the lid. Go shopping. Hit the beach.

1 cross rib roast (4 pounds) or cut of your choice

Salt and pepper to taste

1-1/2 tablespoons minced fresh garlic

All-purpose flour to dust beef

3 tablespoons canola oil

2 medium onions, stew-cut

2 medium carrots, stew-cut

2 medium potatoes, stew-cut

4 stalks celery, stew-cut

1-1/2 quarts chicken broth

1 quart beef broth or enough to cover meat

3/4 cup tomato puree

2 bay leaves

1 sprig rosemary

Mochiko (sweet rice flour) mixed with water to make a thickening agent

Rub salt, pepper and garlic on meat and set aside for a few minutes.

Dust meat with flour. In a large roasting pan, heat oil to medium and then brown meat very well on all sides, about 10 minutes. Add vegetables, broth, and tomato puree. Bring to a boil. Add bay leaves and rosemary.

Cover pan and place in a 350°F oven for 1-1/2 hours or until tender to the fork. Other cuts of meat may take longer, up to 3 or 4 hours depending on the thickness and toughness of the meat.

To make gravy, strain out vegetables from drippings. Bring to a boil and thicken with mochiko diluted with water. Cook and stir until you get the consistency you like. Add back the vegetables.

Traditional Backyard Beef Teriyaki

Serves 4 to 6

You can't go wrong with teriyaki. The flavor brings back a different, happy memory for each of us. This is one thing we can all teach the kids—how to light a hibachi; when the coals are ready—how long to cook the meat. And how wonderful it is to share the meal with family, friends, and neighbors.

Special Teriyaki Glaze (see recipe below)

2 pounds steak of your choice

3 cups soy sauce

2 cups granulated sugar

1/2 cup peeled and minced fresh ginger

4 cloves garlic, minced

4 tablespoons green onions, thinly sliced

1/4 teaspoon white pepper

2 tablespoons minced fresh cilantro

2 teaspoons sesame oil

Slice steak into thin strips and set aside.

Blend remaining ingredients and marinate meat for 4 to 6 hours covered in the refrigerator.

Grill over hot coals (a hibachi seems to make the best flavor) for 2 to 3 minutes on each side, or to desired doneness. The meat is thin, so be careful not to overcook it.

Place meat on a platter and drizzle on Special Teriyaki Glaze.

Special Teriyaki Glaze

Makes about 1 cup

1/2 cup soy sauce

1/4 cup mirin (Japanese sweet rice wine)

1/4 cup water

2 tablespoons brown sugar

1 teaspoon minced fresh garlic

1 teaspoon peeled and minced fresh ginger

1 tablespoon cornstarch mixed with 2 tablespoons water

In a small sauce pan, combine all of the ingredients, except cornstarch mixture. Bring to a boil. Blend cornstarch and water to make a smooth paste. Stir into sauce pan. Reduce heat and simmer, stirring frequently until thickened.

One of my guests on Sam's Kitchen asked me if I ever prepared "Chicken De Loosa." I bit. I said no, is it a difficult recipe? He answered back, "No, it is a bargain dish and very easy. You just go out to the cockfights. De Winna is expensive ... you can get De Loosa for cheap!" That's a good example of the fun that happens in my kitchen. We just don't take it too seriously. We have fun with food.

Next to fresh fish, chicken is probably the most popular protein in Hawai'i. Poultry is healthful food. Minus the skin and the fat, it is versatile and easy to cook. It is forgiving. If you over-cook by a few minutes, it will still be moist; it doesn't ruin easily like shellfish. Use good cooking sense in handling chicken, using it fresh, not re-freezing after defrosting, and cooking it thoroughly. In addition to my favorite roasted chickens, I love to do chicken with fruit or black beans or give it a surprise cinnamon rub.

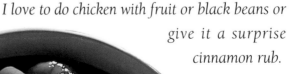

Scene II - Poultry, Pork, Lamb, Turkey and Duck

Nobody Here But Us Chickens & Friends

I use a lot of chicken stock in my cooking. I do make stock from scratch. It has a wonderful aroma as it simmers and you can say homemade is always best. But, when you think of it, all those test kitchens, all the thousands of hours and millions of dollars they spend perfecting a product, the canned, low-sodium chicken stock at the store is pretty good. If you do want to make your own stock use three whole chickens. Just add celery, herbs, and onion. No dark vegetables like carrots or dark onions, you need to keep it light. Other poultry dishes I love to serve include duck, like my Crackling Duck, and oven Kalua-Style Turkey. I sauté many things with sausages, especially Portuguese sausage.

Pork is such an easy meat. It's great with fruit and just about any Island-style marinade. Lamb sometimes scares people. They don't realize how simple a roast leg of lamb can be—and how beautiful it is on the table. Presentation is such a big part of the taste of food. Just that extra minute to add the cilantro or an edible flower or a clean slice of ti leaf. It's worth it!

Braised Chicken

Serves 4

Many people don't know what braising is. When they see it in a recipe, they keep turning the pages. It is actually an easy cooking process that can create a lovely sauce. Here we have seared the meat and then transferred it to a baking dish for a quick trip to the oven.

**1 whole chicken
(about 2-1/2 pounds)**

Vegetable oil for frying

Salt and pepper to taste

2 cups flour to coat chicken

2 onions, julienned

**2 pounds cleaned and quartered fresh
button mushrooms**

**2 cans low-sodium chicken broth
(about 4 cups)**

1/2 teaspoon salt

1/4 teaspoon white pepper

Preheat oven to 350°F.

Cut the chicken in quarters and rinse thoroughly under cold running water. Pat dry. Season chicken with salt and pepper. Dredge each chicken piece in flour. In a large hot skillet or wok, fry the chicken to sear the meat.

Remove chicken from skillet and place in a deep baking pan. Add onions, mushrooms, chicken broth, salt, and pepper to baking pan and cover chicken. Cover pan with aluminum foil. Bake in oven for approximately 30 to 35 minutes.

* Use skinless boneless chicken breasts and place them directly in the baking pan covered with broth and vegetables. This one change lowers the fat by more than 30 grams per serving.

Chicken Chili

Serves 4

*Since Chili-Rice is one of the great "comfort foods" of Hawai'i
it is always nice to have a new, tasty version. This one comes from the Upcountry
cowboy town of Makawao on Maui. The aroma is unbelievable,
the flavor even better.*

2 tablespoons light vegetable oil

**I pound boneless, skinless chicken
thighs, small diced**

I teaspoon Hawaiian salt

I teaspoon fresh ground pepper

I tablespoon minced fresh garlic

1/2 cup diced onions

1/2 cup diced carrots

1/2 cup diced celery

2 tablespoons chili powder

I tablespoon ground cumin

I teaspoon minced fresh oregano

1/2 cup canned chopped tomatoes

1/4 cup tomato paste

**I can (8 ounces) red beans -
drained and rinsed**

**I can (8 ounces) pinto beans -
drained and rinsed**

**I can (8 ounces) black beans -
drained and rinsed**

In a large wok, heat oil to medium-high. Add chicken, salt, pepper, garlic, onions, carrots, and celery and sauté about 2 minutes. Sprinkle chili powder, cumin, and oregano over chicken and vegetables and stir. Mix in tomatoes, tomato paste, and beans and cook about 20 minutes on a low heat.

Serve plain or over cooked rice.

* Use half the oil in a non-stick wok to lower the total fat 3 grams per serving.

Chicken and Coconut Milk

Serves 6

*Canned spinach can be used, along with canned coconut milk.
The chicken can be anything, as long as it is boneless. This is a quick
Hawaiian favorite that can look as if you cooked all day.*

**2 pounds boneless,
skinless chicken**

2 cups coconut milk

**2 cups steamed
spinach (see Note)**

Salt to taste

**I quart low-sodium
chicken broth**

Cut chicken into 2-inch pieces, place
in a pot and cover with chicken broth.
Simmer over low heat for 10 to 15
minutes. Add coconut milk and cook
for 30 minutes or until tender. Add
the cooked and drained spinach; salt
to taste and simmer for 5 minutes.

Note: *2 cups canned or frozen spinach
can be used in place of 2 cups steamed
fresh spinach.*

** By using chicken breast, a low-fat
coconut milk, and a lower fat, low-sodium
chicken broth, you can minimize fat
without compromising flavor.*

Chicken Adobo with Sweet Potatoes

Serves 4

Visit any Filipino family gathering and Adobo will be on the menu. It is a simple dish, flavored with garlic and black pepper. The sweet potatoes add an element of surprise. Yummy when combined with the fried chicken.

2 medium-sized sweet potatoes

2 pounds boneless, skinless chicken thighs

Salt and pepper to taste

1 teaspoon minced fresh garlic

1/2 teaspoon black peppercorn

2 tablespoons soy sauce

1/2 cup vinegar

1 bay leaf

2 tablespoons vegetable oil

Peel and quarter sweet potatoes. Place sweet potatoes and water in a pot and simmer until cooked.

Slice chicken into 1-inch pieces. Add salt, pepper, garlic, peppercorns, and soy sauce. Place in a pan and add bay leaf and vinegar. Cover and simmer until chicken is tender and liquid is evaporated. Add oil and fry chicken until browned. Remove bay leaf. Serve with sweet potatoes.

* Prepare a non-stick pan with a light spray of vegetable oil to lower total fat by more than 5 grams per serving.

Stir-fry Chicken with Fried Noodles

Serves 4

A supermarket stir-fry mix makes this really quick to cook and serve. One tip to remember, use the fresh noodles, cook and remove them quickly— very quickly so they don't turn soggy.

2 tablespoons salad oil

1 pound skinless boneless chicken, diced

1 pound stir-fry mixed vegetables

2 tablespoons soy sauce

2 tablespoons oyster sauce

1 tablespoon minced fresh garlic

1 tablespoon peeled and minced fresh ginger

1 cup low-sodium chicken broth

1 8-ounce package fresh chow mein noodles

1 tablespoon cornstarch mixed with 2 tablespoons water

Garnish:

2 tablespoons green onions, thinly sliced

Heat 2 tablespoons salad oil in large pan and stir-fry the chicken. Cook chicken about 3 to 5 minutes and add mixed vegetables. Stir. Add soy sauce, oyster sauce, garlic, ginger, and chicken broth. Bring to a boil and add the noodles. After about 1 minute, remove noodles and place on a warm platter.

Add the cornstarch mixture to the stir-fry and bring back to a boil. Pour over the noodles and top with green onions. Enjoy!

Cinnamon Chicken   *Serves 4*

Give the chicken a nice Cinnamon Rub. Your taste buds will love you for it.
Put on the pot of rice and begin the sauté. When the chicken is nice and brown it
will be time to add the special flavors of orange juice, raisins, and capers.
Ten minutes later it is done.

**Cinnamon Rub
(see recipe below)**

**4 boneless chicken breast
halves, skin on**

2 tablespoons vegetable oil

3/4 cup chopped onions

Sliced green onions (optional)

2 teaspoons minced fresh garlic

**2 teaspoons peeled and minced
fresh ginger**

**Juice from one orange
(about 3/4 cup)**

2 tablespoons granulated sugar

2 tablespoons raisins

**I tablespoon capers,
rinsed and drained**

Rub cinnamon clove mix into chicken breast. Heat oil in sauté pan over medium-high heat and cook chicken for 3 to 4 minutes, skin side down. Add onions, green onions, garlic, and ginger and stir. Flip chicken breasts over and cook an additional 3 to 4 minutes. Drain off excess oil and add orange juice, sugar, raisins and capers. Reduce heat and simmer approximately 10 minutes.

Cinnamon Rub   *Makes about 1 teaspoon*

I/4 teaspoon ground cinnamon

I/4 teaspoon ground cloves

I/4 teaspoon salt

I/8 teaspoon pepper

Combine ingredients.

Curried Citrus Chicken Papaya

Serves 8

You can't beat fruit with chicken, especially the blended flavors of papaya, citrus, and curry. The frying is quick, then you can relax while the rice cooks and the Curried Citrus Sauce bakes into the boneless chicken meat.

**Curried Citrus Sauce
(see recipe below)**
**3 pounds skinless boneless
chicken thighs**
I cup all-purpose flour
2 teaspoons curry powder
I teaspoon paprika
I teaspoon salt
I teaspoon white pepper
2 tablespoons salad oil
**2 teaspoons peeled and minced
fresh ginger**
2 teaspoons minced fresh garlic
2 teaspoons chopped fresh cilantro

Garnish:

Sliced papaya and citrus fruits
Cilantro

Preheat oven to 350°F.

Combine flour, curry powder, paprika, salt, and white pepper in a large bowl. Dredge chicken in flour mixture and shake off excess. In a large skillet or wok, coat the bottom with salad oil. Pan-fry chicken until golden brown. Place fried chicken in a baking pan, pour Curried Citrus Sauce over the top of the chicken and sprinkle ginger, garlic, and cilantro on top. Bake for 45 minutes. Place on top of a bed of rice and garnish with sliced fruit and cilantro.

* In place of chicken thigh, use skinless boneless chicken breast to reduce the fat.

Curried Citrus Sauce

I-1/2 cups orange juice
2 teaspoons curry powder
I tablespoon cornstarch
1/3 cup brown sugar
2 cups sliced papaya

Makes 1-1/2 cups

Mix ingredients together until sugar is dissolved.

Honey Misoyaki Chicken "Honey Chix"

Serves 4

Boneless chicken thighs are a favorite. Over the coals is the best way to make these sweet-hot "Chix." A 30-minute soak in the marinade is enough and they only take about ten minutes to cook.

**Honey Misoyaki Marinade
(see recipe below)**

8 boneless chicken thighs

Marinate chicken for 30 minutes in the refrigerator.

Meanwhile, prepare grill or heat coals in a hibachi. Grill chicken over coals, turning every 2 to 3 minutes. Total cooking time should be about 8 to 10 minutes. Chicken is done when internal temperature is 170°F.

Honey Misoyaki Marinade

1/2 cup soy sauce
1/2 cup granulated sugar
1/2 cup rice vinegar
5 tablespoons white miso
2/3 cup honey
1 tablespoon chili sauce
1 teaspoon chopped fresh garlic
1 teaspoon chopped fresh cilantro
1/2 cup orange juice

Makes 2-1/2 cups

Mix all ingredients together until sugar is dissolved.

Mango Spiced Chicken

Serves 4

The love affair between fruit and fowl continues. These chickens wear their mango dressing on the outside. A salad of fresh greens with bits of fresh fruit and the usual big bowl of steamed rice makes a perfect meal.

I whole 3- to 4-pound chicken, rinsed and quartered
2 teaspoons Hawaiian salt
I teaspoon white pepper or to taste
2 tablespoons minced fresh garlic
2 tablespoons peeled and grated fresh ginger
Mango Spiced Dressing (see recipe below)

In a bowl, combine salt, white pepper, garlic, and ginger. Rub mixture over chicken and place chicken in covered bowl in refrigerator for a couple of hours.

Preheat oven to 350°F. Place chicken in roasting pan and pour Mango Spiced Dressing over chicken. Bake for 45 to 60 minutes.

*Use skinless boneless chicken breasts instead of the whole chicken and enjoy the leaner version reducing the fat at least 30 grams per serving.

Mango Spiced Dressing

10 ounces Russian salad dressing
8 ounces mango preserves
I package onion soup mix (1-ounce)
I cup peeled and cubed fresh mango
1/4 teaspoon red chili pepper flakes

Makes about 3 Cups

Mix the dressing ingredients together. Set aside.

Macadamia Nut Chicken Breast

Serves 4

These nuts are special to Hawai'i. Dipped in chocolate, topping pie—all of the dessert dishes are what we think of first. But, the mac nut works just great on the main dish. Turning it into a tasty crust for chicken may be its best main dish use!

Minted Pineapple-Papaya Marmalade (see recipe on page 114)

Marinade (see recipe below)

4 boneless chicken breasts (6 ounces each)

1-1/2 cups panko (Japanese-style bread crumbs) or dry bread crumbs

1 cup chopped macadamia nuts

2 tablespoons chopped fresh parsley

1-1/2 cups all-purpose flour

3 whole eggs, whipped

1/2 cup olive oil

Marinate chicken for 30 to 45 minutes.

Meanwhile, mix panko, macadamia nuts, and parsley. Remove chicken from marinade and blot off excess liquid. Dust chicken with flour; dip into whipped eggs and then press the panko-macadamia nut mixture firmly onto chicken.

Lightly coat frying pan with olive oil to cover bottom. Heat oil on medium-high and sauté chicken 3 or 4 minutes on each side until golden brown. Don't overcook. Add more oil as needed. Serve with Minted Pineapple-Papaya Marmalade as a dipping sauce.

Marinade

Makes 1-2/3 cups

1 cup soy sauce

4 tablespoons brown sugar

1 tablespoon peeled and minced fresh ginger

1 tablespoon minced fresh garlic

1/2 cup sherry

Combine marinade ingredients and stir until sugar is dissolved.

Minted Pineapple-Papaya Marmalade

1/2 cup diced papaya
1/2 cup diced pineapple
3 tablespoons granulated sugar
Fresh chopped mint or spearmint

Makes about 1 cup

In a heavy saucepan, combine papaya, pineapple, and sugar; simmer for 20 minutes stirring occasionally. Then add a pinch of fresh chopped mint or spearmint and stir.

Chicken and Egg on Rice Oyako Donburi

Serves 4

Interesting to cook and even more interesting to eat. Make up the Donburi Sauce and boil the heck out of it. The chicken gets a quick dip, then the egg is cooked in a whirlpool. Add fishcake and shiitake mushrooms for an authentic Asian flavor.

4 cups cooked white rice

Donburi Sauce (see recipe below)

8 ounces skinless, boneless chicken, cut into 1/2-inch cubes

2 teaspoons each salt and white pepper

1/2 tablespoon minced fresh garlic

1/2 medium onion, thinly sliced

2 green onions, sliced diagonally

6 eggs, lightly beaten

1/2 cup thinly sliced fishcake

1 cup rinsed and sliced fresh shiitake mushrooms

Prepare white rice.

In a 2-quart pot, heat water to boiling.

Season chicken with salt and pepper. Drop the chicken cubes into boiling water, just until color changes. Transfer immediately to cold water and drain.

To make one serving: Put 1/4 of the Donburi Sauce into a small saucepan. Add 1/4 of the chicken, garlic, and onion and place over high heat. When chicken is done, add green onions. Pour in 1/4 of the egg in a circular pattern to cover as much surface area as possible. When the outer edges of the egg begin to set, stir through once. Put 1 cup of the rice into a deep bowl, fishcake, and slide the egg mixture and the sauce over the rice. Repeat with remaining three servings.

* To lower the fat by 7 grams, just use a prepackaged fat-free egg product.

Donburi Sauce

1-2/3 cups chicken or bonito stock (dashi)

7 tablespoons soy sauce

2 tablespoons mirin (Japanese sweet rice wine)

2 tablespoons granulated sugar

Makes about 2-1/4 cups

Combine the sauce ingredients in a small saucepan and boil over high heat, stirring constantly, until the sugar is dissolved. Set aside.

Chicken with Black Beans

Serves 6

The small, black, fermented soy beans, used in Chinese sauces, are pungent. They are a wonderful gift from Asia but they must be used with a careful hand. The thickened gravy in this dish is perfect over rice or noodles.

2-1/2 pounds boneless chicken thighs (2 thighs per person)

1/8 cup cooked black beans

3 cloves fresh garlic, mashed

1 tablespoon vegetable oil

Pinch of salt

1 tablespoon cornstarch blended with 1 tablespoon water

2 teaspoons granulated sugar

1 tablespoon oyster sauce

Garnish:

Green onions, finely chopped

Cilantro sprigs

Chop chicken thighs in half while still slightly frozen and set aside.

Rinse black beans and then mash beans and mix with garlic. In a large pan, heat oil and add bean mixture. Sauté for 1 to 2 minutes. Add chicken and salt and sauté over medium-high heat, until meat is browned. Cover pan partially and heat until chicken is cooked. To thicken, stir in cornstarch and water mixture. Then add sugar and oyster sauce and cook until gravy thickens. Add more water if necessary. Garnish with green onions and cilantro.

* To decrease total fat per serving by 20 grams and nearly 200 Calories, simply remove the chicken skin.

Shiitake Mushroom Rice
with Shredded Chicken Stir-Fry and Fresh Spinach

Serves 4

Both the chicken and the rice are cooked with full-bodied shiitake mushrooms and onions, adding a lot to the flavor. The wilted spinach is just the right finish to balance the garlic and ginger.

2 cups Basmati rice

2 cups chicken stock or low-sodium chicken broth

1 cup dried shiitake mushroom, rehydrated and sliced

1 cup onion, diced

1 pound skinless, boneless chicken thighs, julienned

1 tablespoon minced fresh garlic

1 tablespoon peeled and minced fresh ginger

1 tablespoon light vegetable oil

3 cups chicken stock or low-sodium chicken broth

1 cup spinach

Salt and white pepper to taste

Garnish:

1 tablespoon chopped green onions

Cook rice with 2 cups chicken stock or as directed on the box. Add to this half of the mushrooms and onions.

Rub chicken with garlic and ginger and let sit about 5 minutes. Heat oil in the wok. Add marinated chicken to wok. Cook about 2 minutes and add remaining mushrooms, onions, and chicken stock. Cook until chicken stock is reduced by half. Add spinach, salt and white pepper to taste. Cook until spinach is wilted.

To serve, pour chicken mushroom mixture over rice.

* This recipe also works well using the lower-fat skinless boneless chicken breast.

Spicy Eggplant with Chicken

*Miso and Japanese rice wine add a tang to the sauce
for the eggplant and chicken. The Asian eggplants work best.
The julienned peppers should add a crisp texture.*

Spicy Eggplant Sauce (see recipe below)

4 tablespoons cooking oil

I clove fresh garlic, crushed

I-inch ginger, crushed

I chili pepper, seeded

1/2 pound skinless, boneless chicken, thinly sliced

5 long Asian eggplants, cut diagonally and soaked in water

2 bell peppers (assorted colors), julienned

2 stalks green onions, cut into I-1/2 inch lengths

2 white onions, julienned

Heat large pan on high and add oil. Fry garlic, ginger, and chili pepper for 1 minute. Remove from pan. Reserve oil.

Add chicken and brown. Pat eggplant dry and add to chicken. Cover pan and cook until eggplant is half done. Add bell peppers and onions. Pour Sauce over mixture. Cook until liquid is almost evaporated, using medium heat throughout.

Spicy Eggplant Sauce:

2 tablespoons soy sauce

2 tablespoons miso (fermented soybean paste)

3 tablespoons brown sugar

I-1/2 tablespoons sake (sweet Japanese rice wine) or sweet sherry

Makes about 1/3 cup

Mix ingredients together until sugar is dissolved.

Chicken and Mahimahi Laulau

Serves 4

Practice is what makes this perfect. Learn how to do a perfect laulau wrap. The layering of the ingredients is the first secret. The second is how they are placed in the criss-crossed ti leaves. And, the third secret is steaming them correctly. They are best served with rice or poi.

I quart water

8 ti leaves

I bunch fresh spinach

4 skinless, boneless chicken breast halves

Salt to taste

4 (3-ounce fillets) mahimahi (dolphinfish), sliced thinly

I cup julienned carrots and zucchini mixture

1/4 cup medium diced sweet potato

1/4 cup medium diced taro

1/4 cup rinsed and julienned fresh shiitake mushrooms

4 slices of tomato

Take 2 medium-sized ti leaves and with a sharp knife remove the ribs. Then with tip of a knife, barely "tap" the rib midway. Pull the rib completely off of two ti leaves. On one of the leaves, split the stem to the bottom of the leaf.

Criss-cross the 2 leaves to make the base of the laulau. Begin layering laulau with spinach leaves, chicken breast, salt, mahimahi fillet, salt, carrot and zucchini mixture, sweet potatoes, taro, shiitake mushrooms and top with a slice of tomato. Pulling the stems up, wrap the split stems around the other two stems and in a knot so that a "pouch" is formed.

Place a steaming rack in a 4 quart pot along with 1/2 to 1-quart of water. Heat until water is at a rapid boil. Carefully place laulau in pot and cover. Steam for approximately 30 to 45 minutes or until done.

Carefully remove laulau and serve with rice or poi.

* Great taste and naturally low in fat.

Haleiwa Barbecued Pork Ribs

Serves 4 to 6

Cook this dish ahead of time, then pack-up the family and the hibachi and head for the park. A quick reheat over the coals and the flavor becomes twice as good. Be sure to make a big batch. Just the effort of eating outside can make you twice as hungry!

Haleiwa Barbecue Sauce (see recipe below)

2 whole slabs pork ribs, cut into sections of 3 ribs each

Water to cover ribs in stockpot

1/2 cup sea salt

4 cloves garlic, whole

1 finger fresh ginger, whole

2 green onions, whole

Place ribs in stockpot and cover with water. Start with 1/2 cup sea salt and keep adding until water tastes salty, then add garlic, ginger, and green onions. Bring to a boil. Reduce heat and let simmer 45 to 60 minutes, or until ribs are tender. Remove ribs from stockpot and let cool.

Heat a hibachi until coals are hot. Brush ribs with barbecue sauce and grill until thoroughly heated. Baste the ribs with barbecue sauce as they cook.

Haleiwa Barbecue Sauce

1 teaspoon red chili flakes

2 cans (15 ounce) tomato sauce

2 cups brown sugar

1/2 cup vinegar

1/2 cup honey

2 cups minced onion

2 teaspoons liquid smoke

2 teaspoons chili powder

1 teaspoon coarsely cracked black pepper

2 tablespoons steak sauce

1/2 teaspoon dry mustard

1 cinnamon stick

1 cup canned crushed pineapple

1 tablespoon minced fresh garlic

Makes about 8 cups

Combine all barbecue sauce ingredients in a saucepan, bring to a boil, reduce heat and simmer 1 hour. Strain.

Pulehu Pork Chops Island-Style

Serves 4

*A little white wine and spices and these chops are ready for the heat.
The hibachi is hot so the logical thing is to make the hibachi vegetables too.
Don't forget to steam the rice!*

Pork Marinade (see recipe below)
8 pork chops (1/2-inch thick)
Hibachi Mixed Vegetables
(see recipe on page 80)

Prepare coals in a hibachi or barbecue grill.

Mix all ingredients together with pork chops. Marinate for 1 hour. Cook over hibachi or barbecue grill. Serve with Hibachi Mixed Vegetables.

Pork Marinade

Makes 1/2 cup

1 tablespoon chopped fresh garlic
1 teaspoon Chili Pepper Water
(see recipe below)
1 teaspoon black pepper
1/4 cup white wine
1/4 cup salad oil

Mix ingredients together.

Chili Pepper Water

Makes 1-1/4 cups

2 Hawaiian chili peppers, minced
1 cup water
1/4 cup vinegar
1 teaspoon Hawaiian salt
1/4 teaspoon fresh garlic, crushed

Combine ingredients in a small sauce pan. Bring water to a simmer and cook for 15 minutes. Set aside.

Mango and Brown Sugar Glazed Pork Chops

Serves 5

Fruit and meat. Mango and pork. They are the perfect match.
This preparation calls for a cooler wok, not a smoking wok. The chops should
be brown, with no pink inside. Add the glaze to finish.

Mango and Brown Sugar Glaze
(see recipe below)
5 pork chops (1/2-inch thick)
6 tablespoons minced fresh garlic
Salt and pepper to taste
Oil for frying

Garnish:
Chopped fresh cilantro

Season pork chop with garlic, salt, and pepper. Lightly oil wok and fry chops on medium-high heat until all pink is gone. Drain on paper towels.

On a platter, place pork chop on the top of a bed of rice. Pour the Mango and Brown Sugar Glaze over the top of the chops and garnish with cilantro.

* Choose a lean chop like a loin chop and cut off the visible fat for the lowest fat.

Mango and Brown Sugar Glaze

Makes 4 cups

1 teaspoon cinnamon
1/2 cup citrus juice
6 tablespoons brown sugar
4 cups julienned fresh mango

Combine ingredients in a saucepan and let simmer until mangos are cooked, about 15 minutes. Set aside

South Pacific Coconut Rice with Sautéed Pork Loin

Serves 3

The coconut rice is topped with what is probably one of the best pestos ever.
Then the tender pork loin is laid on top, and that is covered in fried onions. 'Ono!

**4 tablespoons Ginger Pesto
(see recipe below)**

4 cups Basmati rice

2 cups coconut milk

**2 cups chicken stock or
low-sodium chicken broth**

**1/4 cup light vegetable oil plus
2 tablespoons oil**

1 cup diced onions

1 cup all-purpose flour

Pinch of salt and pepper

**6 pieces pork loin
(2-1/2 ounces each)**

Garnish:

1/2 cup thinly sliced fried onions

Cook rice with coconut milk and stock. Cook as if using only water. When rice is cooked, dollop with a little ginger pesto.

Meanwhile, heat 1/4 cup salad oil in a wok. Dust onions with flour, salt, and pepper. Shake off all excess flour and fry in oil until golden brown. Remove and place on paper towel to drain.

In a separate wok, heat remaining 1 tablespoon of oil. Dust pork with flour, salt, and pepper. Cook in hot oil about 2 minutes on each side. Serve over rice with fried onions on top of pork.

** Use low-fat coconut milk to lower fat about
30 grams.*

Ginger Pesto

1 teaspoon salt

1/2 cup peeled and minced fresh ginger

1/2 cup minced green onions

**1/2 cup lightly packed minced fresh
cilantro**

1/4 teaspoon white pepper

1 cup salad oil

Makes about 2 cups

In a large mixing bowl, combine all ingredients for the pesto except for the salad oil. Mix thoroughly with a wire whisk. Gradually add salad oil while continually whisking until all oil is incorporated.

Teriyaki Lamb Chops with Dijon Mustard Crust

Serves 4

Let the lamb marinate for six hours, or even overnight. The homemade teriyaki sauce and Japanese panko crispy bread crumbs combined with macadamia nuts give this dish a real Island flavor. Remember, lamb chops are best when they are not well done.

**Teriyaki Sauce
(see recipe below)**

16 lamb chops

4 tablespoons garlic chili sauce

**2 cups macadamia nuts,
finely chopped**

**1-1/2 cups panko (Japanese-
style crispy bread crumbs)
or fine dried bread crumbs**

2 cups spicy Dijon mustard

1 tablespoon vegetable oil

Marinate lamb in Teriyaki Sauce for 4 to 6 hours in refrigerator.

Combine macadamia nuts and panko. Set aside.

Remove chops and brush both sides of each lamb chop with spicy Dijon mustard and roll in crust mixture. In a heavy skillet, with a little oil over medium heat, sear lamb chops on both sides, turning until desired doneness is reached. Set aside and cool.

Teriyaki Sauce

Makes about 8-1/2 cups

4 cups soy sauce

**2 cups mirin (Japanese
sweet rice wine)**

2 cups water

1 cup brown sugar

2 tablespoons minced fresh garlic

**2 tablespoons peeled and
minced fresh ginger**

2 tablespoons garlic chili sauce

6 tablespoons sliced green onions

Mix ingredients until sugar dissolves.

GALLO *of* SONOMA
SONOMA COUNTY
Cabernet Sauvignon

BARREL AGED

1997

ALC. 13.5% BY VOL.

Oriental Lamb Chops with Rotelli pasta

Serves 4 to 6

One of the most popular dishes in the Sam Choy restaurants, this recipe combines the Italian with the Asian. The pasta, drenched in the cream sauce, makes the perfect bed for the marinated chops.

Creamy Rotelli Pasta (see recipe below)
1/2 cup soy sauce
3/4 cup minced fresh garlic
1 tablespoon peeled and minced fresh ginger
2 cups brown sugar
1/2 teaspoon red chili pepper flakes
1/2 cup minced fresh basil
1/2 cup minced fresh cilantro
Salt to taste
8 to 12 lamb chops (2 to 3 per person)

Combine soy sauce, garlic, ginger, brown sugar, chili pepper, basil, cilantro, and salt. Massage into meat for 5 to 10 minutes, then let marinate 4 to 6 hours in refrigerator.

Prepare Rotelli Pasta accordingly. Heat broiler and broil chops to perfection (about 2 to 3 minutes per side for medium rare, or to your liking). Serve 2 or 3 chops over a bed of pasta.

Creamy Rotelli Pasta

Serves 4

2 tablespoons butter
4 tablespoons olive oil
1-1/2 tablespoons minced fresh garlic
1 medium carrot, julienned
2 medium zucchini, julienned
2 cups rinsed and julienned shiitake mushrooms
2 cup coarsely chopped cilantro
12 ounces rotelli
1-1/2 cups heavy cream
Salt and pepper to taste
3/4 cup grated Parmesan cheese

Cook pasta according to package directions; drain and set aside.

In a large saucepan, heat butter and olive oil over medium-high heat. Sauté garlic for about 1 minute. And vegetables and stir-fry for 2 to 3 minutes. Add drained pasta and stir fry another minute. Add heavy cream, bring to a boil and immediately reduce to a simmer. Adjust seasoning with salt and pepper. Just before serving, add Parmesan cheese and let cook one minute.

Roast Pork Loin with Goat Cheese Water Chestnut Filling

Serves 8

This is a meal for the "royal family"— your own!
The goat cheese and spinach melt into a beautiful flavor to stuff the pork loin.
The roast cooks on a bed of onions, celery, and carrots. The pan juices
are so good you could almost drink them.

Goat Cheese Filling (see recipe below)

5 pounds pork loin

1 large round onion

2 celery stalks, chunked

2 carrots, chunked

2 tablespoons soy sauce

1 tablespoon peeled and minced fresh garlic

Preheat oven to 350°F. With a sharp knife, cut pork loin creating a hole through the center to add Goat Cheese Filling. Stuff filling into center of pork loin. With butcher's string, tie netting around the roast.

Place pork loin on a bed of onions, celery, and carrots. Top loin with soy sauce and minced garlic. Season top of roast with salt and pepper. Bake for 1-1/2 hours.

*Serve smaller portions, but accompany it with lots of steamed vegetables or even applesauce.

Goat Cheese Filling

2 tablespoons peeled and minced fresh garlic

1-1/2 cups sliced round onion

1 cup sliced celery

1/2 cup fresh spinach leaves, rinsed and drained

Salt and pepper to taste

2 cups rinsed and sliced fresh shiitake mushrooms

1 can (8-ounce) water chestnuts, drained, rinsed, and sliced

1 cup crumbled goat cheese

Makes about 5 cups

In a wok, combine garlic, onions, and celery. Add spinach and season with salt and pepper. Add mushrooms and water chestnuts. When vegetables are almost cooked, add goat cheese and mix well.

BBQ Pork Tenderloin with Garlic Sauce

Serves 6

OK, for this one you need to love garlic like Sam does. This roast could be done in an oven, but the hibachi is best. When the meat is done, let it rest. Slice and top with the macadamia nuts and the Garlic Sauce.

Barbecue Marinade (see recipe on page 130)

Garlic Sauce (see recipe on page 130)

3 pounds pork tenderloin

2 tablespoons minced fresh garlic

2 tablespoons peeled and grated fresh ginger

1 teaspoon salt

1/2 teaspoon white pepper

Garnish:

Chopped macadamia nuts

Season pork with garlic, ginger, salt, and white pepper, then brush on Barbecue Marinade. Be sure that entire surface of pork is covered with the marinade. Marinate pork for 1 hour in refrigerator.

Prepare barbecue grill or coals in a hibachi.

Grill pork over medium-high heat and brush with residual marinade frequently until the minimum internal pork temperature is 150°F. Let tenderloin rest for 5 to 10 minutes before slicing.

To plate, serve with garlic sauce over pork slices and garnish with macadamia nuts. Brown in oven if desired.

Barbecue Marinade

**2 tablespoons hoisin sauce
(sweet-spicy soybean-garlic sauce)**

2 tablespoons catsup

2 tablespoons soy sauce

1 teaspoon granulated sugar

Makes 1/3 Cup

Combine and mix well until sugar dissolves.

Garlic Sauce

6 tablespoons soy sauce

2 tablespoons minced fresh garlic

**1 tablespoon mirin (Japanese sweet
rice wine)**

1 tablespoon granulated sugar

1 tablespoon chili oil

1 tablespoon minced fresh cilantro

Makes 3/4 cup

Mix all ingredients until sugar dissolves.

Roast Leg of Lamb,
Portuguese Sausage Sweet Bread Stuffing, Green Beans, and Garlic-Jalapeño Mint Jam

Serves 6 to 8

This dish looks wonderful when it is served. Using netting and string helps the presentation. The overnight marinade is the secret to the juicy, rich flavor. Don't be afraid. If you follow this step-by-step, you will have perfection the first time out.

Lamb Marinade (see recipe below)

Portuguese Sausage Sweet Bread Stuffing (see recipe on page 132)

Green Beans (see recipe on page 132)

Garlic-Jalapeño Mint Jam (see recipe on page 132)

1 boneless leg of lamb (about 5 pounds), netted

1/2 cup large diced celery

1 onion, large diced

1/2 cup large diced carrot

Rub marinade all over the lamb and let marinate overnight in the refrigerator. Preheat oven to 325°F. Stuff filling into center of lamb. With butcher's string, tie netting around the roast. Place diced vegetables in roasting pan and place the lamb on top. Bake for about 1-1/2 to 2 hours.

Lamb Marinade

1 cup soy sauce

1 cup brown sugar

1 tablespoon peeled and minced fresh ginger

1 tablespoon minced fresh garlic

1 teaspoon red chili pepper flakes

1 tablespoon sesame oil

Makes about 1-1/2 cups

Combine soy sauce, brown sugar, ginger, garlic, chili flakes, and sesame oil; blend together.

Portuguese Sausage Sweet Bread Stuffing

Makes about 8 cups

*Stuffing is great with just about any meat dish. Serve it whenever
a very tasty starch would add something different to the meal. This combo of
Portuguese sausage and Portuguese sweet bread is always a favorite.*

2 sticks (1/2 pound) butter
1 pound bacon, diced
1 pound Portuguese sausage, diced
2 cups diced onions
1 cup diced celery
2 cups diced Portuguese
sweet bread
Beef or chicken stock as necessary
Salt, pepper, and fresh thyme to taste

Add butter and bacon to large pan. Let them start to render. Stir in sausage and vegetables. Cook until onions are translucent; add stock and stir together. Add diced and toasted sweet bread to desired consistency. Add more stock for a wetter stuffing.

Garlic-Jalapeño Mint Jam

Makes about 3 cups

1 pound brown sugar
1 pound butter
10 cloves whole garlic, peeled
3 red jalapeño peppers, minced
1 bunch fresh mint, chopped
(about 1 cup)

Over medium heat, combine sugar, butter, and garlic. Stir until sugar and butter are melted together and garlic reaches a caramel stage about 5 to 6 minutes. Add jalapeño peppers and mint. Stir well and reserve in jars.

Green Beans

Makes 4 cups

1 pound green beans, rinsed, trimmed,
and cut into 1-inch lengths
1/4 cup bacon bits
1/2 cup diced red bell peppers
Salt and pepper to taste

In a wok or skillet, melt butter and add green beans. Stir-fry until half cooked, then add bacon bits and diced pepper. Season with salt and pepper to taste.

Kalua-Style Turkey
with Dried Fruit & Oyster Stuffing and Baked Taro and Sweet Potato

Serves 12

No need to dig up the front lawn, this kalua turkey does just fine in the oven. The stuffing is a "Sam special." Serve it with the baked taro and sweet potato and you have real holiday feast.

Dried Fruit & Oyster Stuffing
(see recipe on page 134)

Baked Taro and Sweet Potatoes
(see recipe on page 135)

1 whole turkey with giblets
(about 15 pounds)

Hawaiian salt to taste

1/4 cup soy sauce

2 tablespoons liquid smoke

2 quarts chicken stock or
low-sodium chicken broth

10 medium-size ti leaves

Preheat oven at 350°F.

Wash turkey, pat dry inside and out. Rub with soy sauce and season generously with salt and pepper. Place half the ti leaves in a roasting pan, add liquid smoke and chicken stock to the pan, add the turkey, breast down, to the pan and cover with remaining ti leaves. Seal pan very well with foil. Bake for about 4 hours or until done (depending on turkey size). After turkey cools, shred the meat off the bone.

Dried Fruit & Oyster Stuffing | *Makes about 8 cups*

Begin with bacon for flavor and for the great aroma of the bacon and the onions cooking in the pan. Add several dried fruits. Cranberries add the festive look. The oysters should be poached a bit then added in. The sweet bread gives 'ono flavor.

1/4 pound bacon
1/4 cup onion, chopped
1/4 cup carrots, chopped
1/4 cup celery, chopped
1/4 cup peeled garlic cloves
1/4 cup minced fresh thyme
Turkey giblets
1 pound assorted dried fruit (cranberry, mango, papaya)
1 quart chicken stock or low-sodium chicken broth
1 quart oyster meat in juice
2 cups toasted Hawaiian sweet bread cubes (about 1/2-inch pieces)
Salt and pepper to taste

Render the bacon and sauté the onion, carrots, celery, garlic, and thyme. When vegetables are cooked, add the giblets and dried fruits. Cook for 5 minutes. Add the chicken stock and oysters (lightly poach oyster meat in juice before adding to stock). When hot, add the sweet bread (for a dryer stuffing add less stock). Cook until all the liquid is absorbed, season with salt and pepper to taste.

Baked Taro and Sweet Potatoes | *Makes about 12 cups*

This dish is good any time of year. Butter the pan, layer the taro and sweet potato, dot with more butter. Add raisins, more butter, macadamia nuts and more butter. Drizzle with coconut syrup and add just a bit more butter!

1 pound whole butter
3 pounds taro, peeled and thinly sliced
3 pounds sweet potato, peeled and thinly sliced
1/2 cup packed brown sugar
1 cup raisins
Salt and pepper to taste
1/2 cup all-purpose flour
1/2 cup chopped macadamia nuts
4 ounces coconut syrup

Preheat oven to 350°F. Rub a casserole dish with butter and layer the taro and sweet potatoes, dotting with butter, brown sugar, raisins, salt and pepper. When done, combine the flour, macadamia nuts, butter, and coconut syrup until it is dry and resembles crumbly pie dough. When taro and sweet potato are done, top with the macadamia nut mixture and bake until it is golden brown. Bake for 30 to 40 minutes.

Sam Choy's Award-Winning Roast Duck

Serves 4 to 6

*This "people's award" winning dish is much easier than it seems.
A traditional Chinese roast duck takes lots of time. This simple short-cut
recipe offers all the taste in half the time.*

2 ducks (3 to 4 pounds each)
3/4 cup soy sauce
I tablespoon salt
I tablespoon garlic salt
I teaspoon garlic powder
I teaspoon paprika
1/2 teaspoon white pepper
I tablespoon coriander seeds (whole)

Remove wing tips, neck flap, tail end, excess fat, and drumstick knuckles. Rinse both ducks. Place in a dish, and pour soy sauce over them. Roll the ducks in the soy sauce and let sit for about 20 minutes. Keep rolling in the soy sauce every 3 to 4 minutes.

Preheat oven to 550°F.

Mix remaining ingredients to make a dry marinade. Place duck breast side up on rack in a roasting pan and sprinkle thoroughly with marinade. Also, put a little marinade inside cavities.

Roast for 30 minutes. Reduce heat to 325°F. Cook for 1 hour or until meat thermometer registers an internal temperature of 170 to 175°F. No basting is necessary.

Serve with steamed rice.

Crackling Duck with Vegetables

Serves 4

*This duck is deep-fried until the skin "crackles."
When it is cool, the bones come out and the duck goes for a swim in the
marinade of citrus, ginger and garlic. Make the stir-fry vegetables
into a nest for the duck then "crown him" with edible flowers.*

**Crackling Duck Dressing
(see recipe below)
I whole duck (5 pounds)
I teaspoon red chili pepper flakes
Salt and white pepper to taste
1/2 cup flour/cornstarch mixture (50/50)
Peanut oil for deep-frying
1/2 cup whole Chinese snow peas
1/2 cup rinsed and sliced fresh shiitake
mushrooms
1/2 cup julienned carrots
I cup straw mushrooms
I red pepper, julienned
I cup bean sprouts
I tablespoon salad oil
2 teaspoons minced fresh garlic
2 teaspoons peeled and minced
fresh ginger
Salt and pepper to taste**

Garnish:

**I apple, diced, and edible flowers
(pansies and nasturtiums)**

Season duck with hot pepper flakes, salt, and pepper. Dust with flour/cornstarch mixture. Deep-fry in peanut oil until golden brown. Drain on paper towels. Remove bones when cool. Marinate deep-fried duck in Crackling Duck Dressing and toss lightly.

Stir-fry vegetables with salad oil, garlic, ginger, salt, and pepper, until al dente.

Line bowls with vegetables and top with duck, diced apple, and edible flowers.

Crackling Duck Dressing

**I-1/2 cups orange juice
1/2 cup soy sauce
1/2 cup balsamic vinegar
1/2 tablespoon minced fresh garlic
I teaspoon peeled and minced
fresh ginger
2 cups brown sugar
Hot red chili pepper flakes to taste**

Makes 2 cups

Mix ingredients together until sugar is dissolved.

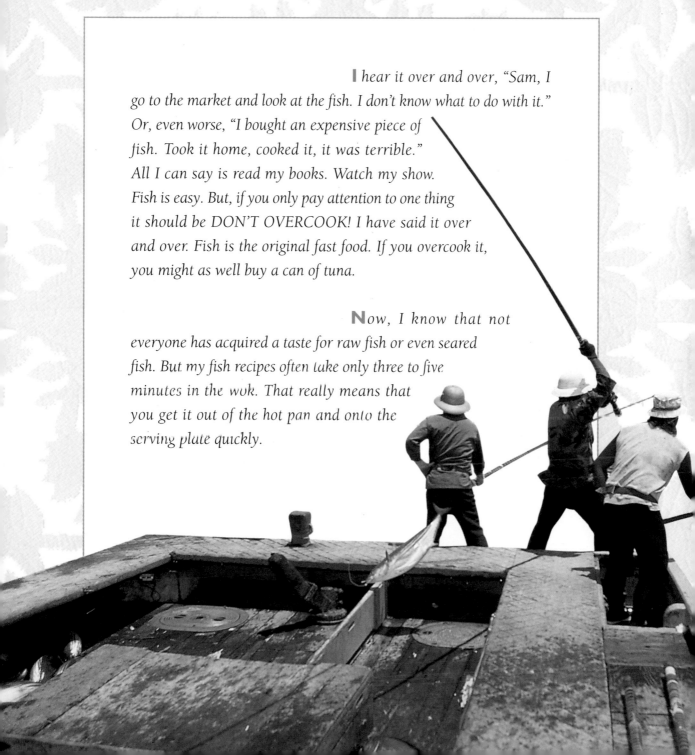

Scene III - Fish

Ladies & Gentlemen,
May I Present the First Fish

I hear it over and over, "Sam, I go to the market and look at the fish. I don't know what to do with it." Or, even worse, "I bought an expensive piece of fish. Took it home, cooked it, it was terrible." All I can say is read my books. Watch my show. Fish is easy. But, if you only pay attention to one thing it should be DON'T OVERCOOK! I have said it over and over. Fish is the original fast food. If you overcook it, you might as well buy a can of tuna.

Now, I know that not everyone has acquired a taste for raw fish or even seared fish. But my fish recipes often take only three to five minutes in the wok. That really means that you get it out of the hot pan and onto the serving plate quickly.

If you want to start out with a nearly fool-proof fish, try Mahimahi. You can actually overcook this fish and it will still be moist. It is versatile. Make my mahimahi crusted with macadamia nuts or the Mahimahi with Warm Corn Sauce and Green Fried Tomatoes and you'll be a hero.

Buy fish from a reputable market. Make sure the case is well chilled. Watch the color of the fish. Ask questions. There are many great Hawaiian fishes for sale, and dozens of preparations for each one. This is where you turn back to that inner circle of flavors. If you love the Asian flavor use Thai chili or black bean. Don't be afraid to fry or wok in oil. It is true that you shouldn't have fried foods every day, but there isn't anything better than a crisp Pan Fried Mullet. Watch the show, you'll see that many of the fishes make an easy sauce as they cook.

Fish is a quick, delicious dinner.

Sam Choy's Big Aloha Fried Poke Wrap

Serves 1

A South-of-the-border tortilla turns multi-ethnic when it's folded around Portuguese fried rice, fried Hawaiian swordfish poke and topped with an oriental dressing and Wasabi Mayonnaise.

Wasabi Mayonnaise (see recipe below)

1 cup Fried Rice (see recipe on page 143)

5 ounces Fried Poke (see recipe on page 143)

1 wrap-size taro flavored flour tortilla (12-inches)

1/4 cup Sam Choy's Creamy Oriental Dressing

1/8 cup shredded greens, such as romaine or iceberg lettuce

Place a pinch of salt in a large, heavy skillet and briefly heat tortilla wrap on both sides (15 seconds each). Place tortilla on a plate and layer shredded greens, Fried Rice, and Fried Poke onto the tortilla wrap. Add Wasabi Mayonnaise and oriental dressing to taste. Roll tortilla wrap and eat!

* Use Sam Choy's Reduced Fat, Reduced Calorie Creamy Oriental Dressing.

Wasabi Mayonnaise

Makes 1-1/3 cups

2 tablespoons wasabi powder

4 tablespoons water

1 cup mayonnaise

Make a paste with wasabi powder and water. Mix into mayonnaise to make a smooth creamy paste. Season with a pinch of salt and pepper.

* In place of 1 cup mayonnaise, use 1/3 cup mayonnaise and 2/3 non-fat mayonnaise.

GALLO *of* SONOMA
RUSSIAN RIVER VALLEY
Pinot Noir
BARREL AGED   *1998*

Fried Rice

1/4 cup diced bacon, spam, or Portuguese sausage

1 egg, scrambled

1 tablespoon chopped green onions

1 tablespoon oyster sauce

1 teaspoon sesame oil

1 cup cooked rice

Makes 1-1/3 cups

Sauté breakfast meat for about 2 minutes, add scrambled egg and keep stirring until eggs are cooked. Add rice, oyster sauce, sesame oil and combine until mixed well. Finish with green onions, mix thoroughly.

Fried Poke

7 ounces swordfish cut into 1/2-inch cubes

1/3 cup medium diced white onions

1/3 cup sliced green onions

1/2 cup rinsed and chopped ogo seaweed

1-1/2 tablespoons soy sauce

1/2 teaspoon Hawaiian salt

3 drops sesame oil

Sam Choy's Big Aloha Beer or other beer (optional marinade)

Makes about 2 cups

Heat wok to medium-high. Combine all ingredients, except beer, in a bowl and mix well. Quickly fry poke in wok and set aside. Marinate with beer to taste if desired.

Green Papaya Chanpuru

Serves 4

Tuna and tofu together are a power pack. Do a wok browning on the tofu. Add the tuna and get ready with the rice. Great taste is added with the bonito broth and mirin wine mixture.

1/4 cup canola oil

20 ounces firm tofu, drained

1/8 teaspoon sea salt or Hawaiian salt

1/2 green papaya, skinned and coarsely grated

1/2 cup coarsely grated carrots

1 thinly sliced round onion

2 tablespoons canned tuna

1/2 cup low-sodium chicken broth or bonito broth

1/2 teaspoon mirin (Japanese sweet rice wine)

1/8 teaspoon sesame oil

1/8 teaspoon soy sauce

Heat canola oil in large skillet or wok. Add hand-broken tofu pieces and sprinkle salt over tofu. Brown tofu pieces thoroughly. Add green papaya, carrots, onions, and tuna. Stir-fry.

In a separate saucepan, bring broth to boil and add to skillet. Season to taste with mirin, soy sauce, and sesame oil. Do not overcook vegetables.

Deep-Fried Kali Kali* Fish with Tropical Fruit Salsa

Serves 4

This time the snapper is deep-fried whole. The shallow cuts on the sides allow the fish to cook evenly with crispy skin. Make the Tropical Fruit Salsa first so the flavors will meld together while the fish is cooking. The melons, pineapple, and papaya should be chopped about the same size. Mixing in the corn and beans makes a really unusual flavor.

Tropical Fruit Salsa (see recipe below)

4 kali kali (about 1-1/2 pounds each)

2 -1/2 cups flour

Salt and pepper to taste

3 cups salad oil

In a wok or deep heavy pot, heat oil to 365°F. Score the fish on both sides by making shallow cuts in the surface of the fish. Roll the fish in flour and deep-fry until fish is cooked.

To serve, place one fish per platter and top with Tropical Fruit Salsa.

Tropical Fruit Salsa

1/4 cup diced honeydew melon

1/4 cup diced cantaloupe

1/4 cup diced pineapple

1/4 cup diced papaya

1/4 cup fresh corn

1/4 cup cooked black beans

1/4 cup cooked white beans

1 tablespoon chopped red onions

1 tablespoon chopped round onion

1 cup honey

1 tablespoon soy sauce

1 cup orange juice

1/4 cup cider vinegar

Salt and pepper to taste

Makes about 2 cups

Mix ingredients together in a large mixing bowl, add marinade and toss everything together.

* Also known as kale kale (snapper)

Steamed 'Opakapaka
with Pink Pickled Ginger and Red Onion

Serves 4

The very popular 'Opakapaka is a pink or crimson snapper with firm light-pink flesh. Its firmness makes it especially good for steaming. Fill the rice cooker and get the chopping done. Then steam the fish. The pickled ginger, garlic chili sauce, fresh garlic and ginger, and lemon juice infuse the broth with incredible flavor.

2 pounds whole 'opakapaka (pink snapper)

I tablespoon minced fresh garlic

I tablespoon peeled and minced fresh ginger

1/4 cup chopped red onions

I tablespoon garlic chili sauce

1/4 cup pink pickled ginger slices

Salt to taste

I cup fresh lemon juice

1/2 cup bean sprouts

1/2 cup rinsed and chopped watercress

Fill the base pot of a tiered aluminum steamer with about 1/3 water. Cover and bring to a boil over medium-high heat.

Put 'opakapaka in a deep heat-proof bowl and arrange the remaining ingredients on top. (The bowl should fit in a steamer rack with at least 1-inch of clearance all around.)

Set the bowl with the ingredients in the middle of the steamer rack. When the water reaches a boil, set the rack over the pot. Cover and steam until 'opakapaka is cooked through and the herbs have infused the broth, about 18 to 20 minutes.

Transfer the fish with all the aromatic broth to a deep serving platter or a covered casserole. Serve with plenty of steamed rice.

GALLO *of* SONOMA
RUSSIAN RIVER VALLEY
Chardonnay
BARREL FERMENTED
1998

Sesame Crusted 'Ahi with Vegetable Trio with Chinese Vinaigrette and Curry Oil

It's possible that Seared 'Ahi is on every restaurant menu in the State. Cook it at home. You can have "real size" servings and seconds when you want. The vinaigrette and curry oil are a nice change from the usual wasabi.

Curry Oil (see recipe below)
Chinese Vinaigrette (see recipe below)
1/4 cup black sesame seeds
1/4 cup white sesame seeds
4 blocks fresh 'ahi (yellowfin tuna), 4 ounces each (1 x 1 x 3-inch blocks)
2 tablespoons chili pepper water (see recipe on page 122)
1 cup julienned daikon (white radish)
1 cup julienned carrot
1 cup julienned cucumber

Mix sesame seeds and place in a shallow bowl.

Rub 'ahi with chili pepper water then roll in mixture of both sesame seeds. Heat pan and sear each side, leaving inside rare.

Mix daikon, carrot, and cucumber with Chinese Vinaigrette.

Slice each 'ahi block into 3 lengthwise pieces and place pieces on a plate, forming a triangle point. Place vegetables in middle of plate. Drizzle both Chinese Vinaigrette and Curry Oil around plate.

Chinese Vinaigrette

1/2 cup black vinegar
1/2 cup curry oil (see below)
Salt and pepper to taste

Makes 1 cup

Combine ingredients and whip to emulsify.

Curry Oil

4 tablespoons curry powder
1 cup salad oil

Makes 1-1/4 cups

Combine ingredients in saucepan and heat for 20 minutes, then let sit for one hour.

Louisiana Style Bar-B-Que
"Sam's Walk into the Wok"

Serves 4

Caramelized onion coats the wok. Two kinds of shrimp, 'ahi, scallops and great spices jump in next. Then heavy cream and butter simmer into a creamy sauce. Garlic bread is perfect to soak up the sauce when your plate is empty!

I pound fillet of fresh 'ahi (yellowfin tuna)
cut into 3/4-inch cubes

I cup rock shrimp, peeled and deveined

8 scallops, rinsed and drained

8 tiger shrimp, peeled and deveined

3 teaspoons salt

3 teaspoons cayenne pepper

2 teaspoons cracked black pepper

I tablespoon olive oil

I medium round onion, chopped

2 tablespoons minced fresh garlic

Juice from 3 lemons
(about 6 tablespoons)

I tablespoon Worcestershire sauce

1/2 teaspoon Tabasco sauce

3/4 cup heavy cream

3 tablespoons butter

Garnish:

Garlic bread

2 stalks green onions
cut into 1/2-inch strips

In a large bowl, mix together and season seafood with 2 teaspoons each of salt, cayenne pepper, and cracked black pepper. Set aside.

Using a large wok or skillet, heat olive oil to a medium-low heat and add the chopped round onion. Sprinkle over the onion the remaining salt and cayenne pepper and stir until onion is caramelized.

Increase wok temperature to medium-high and add seafood and remaining ingredients, except butter. Let the seafood simmer, but do not overcook. Add butter and stir. When butter melts this dish is ready to serve.

Serve on a platter with garlic bread and garnish with green onion strips.

* Use half and half instead of cream and decrease butter to 2 tablespoons to maintain the flavor but lower total fat by 10 grams per serving.

Baked Citrus Crusted Onaga

Serves 4

Japanese red snapper keeps its skin on while it bakes in a butter-citrus mixture. Preparing the zest for the fruits is well worth the effort. The aroma will draw everyone to the kitchen where they will just wait for you to put it on the table.

Zest from lime, orange, and lemon

2 tablespoons butter

Juice of 1 lime (about 1 tablespoon)

Juice of 1/2 orange (about 4 tablespoons)

Juice of 1/2 lemon (about 1 tablespoon)

1 teaspoon Worcestershire sauce

Vegetable pan spray (like Pam)

4 fresh onaga fillets, 6-ounces each (with skin)

1/4 cup dry bread crumbs or panko (Japanese-style bread crumbs)

Salt and pepper to taste

Preheat oven to 400°F.

Remove the zests from lime, orange, and lemon using a citrus zester. In a small sauce pan, combine butter, lime, lemon, orange juices, the zest of all three citrus fruits, and Worcestershire sauce. Heat pan until juices sizzle. Remove from heat.

Prepare baking pan with vegetable oil spray. Season fish on both sides with salt and pepper. Place fish, skin side down, and pour butter-citrus mixture over the fish. Top with bread crumbs. Bake for 8 to 10 minutes or until done.

Sautéed Onaga
with Kabocha Squash Sauce and Braised Watercress

Serves 4

Another picture-perfect dish. The pink meat of the sautéed onaga, sautéed quickly, rests on a green bed of watercress. Each plate is turned into a painter's palette with the Red Pepper Coulis on one side and the squash sauce on the other. Beautiful!

Red Pepper Coulis (see recipe on page 153)

Kabocha Squash Sauce (see recipe on page 153)

4 onaga (red snapper) fillets (4-ounces each)

Salt and pepper to taste

1/2 cup rinsed watercress, fresh cut into 1 inch segments

8 tablespoons (1/4 pound) unsalted butter

Garnish:

8 zucchini blossoms

Cut fish into 4-ounce pieces and season with salt and pepper. Add a touch of butter to the sauté pan. Cook each side for 2 minutes on medium heat. Add 2 tablespoons butter and watercress to sauté pan on medium heat just until it wilts.

Place watercress in the center of the plate. Place the onaga on top of the watercress. Decorate with the Red Pepper Coulis and Kabocha Squash Sauce and garnish with 2 zucchini blossoms each.

Red Pepper Coulis

2 red bell peppers, medium diced
4 shallots, medium diced
2-3 ounces vermouth
6 ounces white wine
2 ounces Dry Sack sherry
Salt and pepper to taste

Makes about 1-1/2 cups

Split red pepper in half and take out the seeds. In a sauce pan, add the red peppers, shallots, 2 to 3 ounces of white wine and vermouth, and 1 sprig of thyme. Boil for 25 minutes.

Purée and strain, and season with salt, pepper and sherry. Keep warm.

Kabocha Squash Sauce

I each Kabocha squash
(6" diameter)
Salt and pepper to taste
I teaspoon fresh thyme leaves
I cup heavy cream

Makes 3 to 4 cups

Cut the squash in half and take out the seeds. Peel all the green outer skin off and medium dice.

In a medium-size sauce pan, place kabocha and cover with water. Add salt, pepper, and thyme leaves. Bring to a boil and simmer for 20 minutes. Purée squash and add cream. Strain, and keep warm.

* Replace heavy cream with half and half to lower total fat by 60 grams.

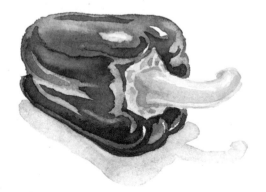

Pan Fried Mullet

Serves 2

*Simple. Just a mullet fish and a package of chop suey mix.
Wok the fish then sauté the vegetables, creating the sauce at the same time.
Pour over the fish and there you have it, a feast.*

1/4 cup salad oil for frying

1 pound whole mullet

Salt and pepper to taste

**2 tablespoons peeled and minced
fresh ginger**

1 cup all-purpose flour

**1 package (9-ounces) chop suey
vegetable mix**

1 cup low-sodium chicken broth

4 tablespoons soy sauce

4 tablespoons oyster sauce

**1 tablespoon cornstarch mixed with
2 tablespoons water**

Garnish:

**2 tablespoons thinly sliced
green onions**

Heat oil in a wok or deep-frying pan until smoking.

Score the mullet on both sides (cut 1/2-inch deep cuts every inch) and season with salt, pepper, and ginger. Dust mullet in flour and place seasoned mullet in hot oil and cook about 4 minutes on each side. Remove from pan and set aside.

Drain all but 2 tablespoons of oil from pan. Add chop suey mix to pan. Add chicken broth, soy sauce, oyster sauce and bring to a boil. Thicken with cornstarch.

Pour vegetables and sauce over fish and top with green onions. Enjoy!

Sautéed Island Fish Trio

Serves 4

*Mahi, 'ahi and 'opakapaka are favorites. Separate, they are delicious.
Put them together and they present a flavor combination made in heaven.
The cream and mushroom sauce surrounds them in a lush, rich pool.*

Trio Sauce (see recipe below)
5 cups julienned vegetables (see **Note**)
5 tablespoons butter
3 tablespoons olive oil
1/2 teaspoon garlic, minced
Salt and pepper to taste
4 (2-ounce fillets) 'opakapaka (pink snapper)
4 (2-ounce fillets) mahimahi (dolphinfish)
4 (2-ounce fillets) 'ahi (yellowfin tuna)
1/2 cup flour to dust fish

Garnish:

4 sprigs of fresh parsley, or sprigs of your favorite fresh herbs

Trio Sauce:

1 tablespoon soy sauce
2 cups heavy cream
1 tablespoon ginger, minced
1 cup shiitake mushrooms, sliced
salt and pepper to taste

Heat 2 tablespoons butter and 1 tablespoon olive oil and sauté vegetables and garlic for 2 minutes. Season with salt and pepper. Remove from pan, set aside and keep warm.

Lightly season fish with salt and pepper and dust with flour. Heat 3 tablespoons butter and 2 tablespoons olive oil in large sauté pan. Cook fish until medium rare, about 1-1/2 minutes per side.

Divide vegetables into 4 equal portions and mound 1 portion in the middle of each plate. Arrange 1 plate filled with each of the three different types of island fish around the side of the vegetable mound in a sort of pyramid fashion. Pour sauce around the edge and garnish with a sprig of parsley or other fresh herbs.

Makes 1 to 2 cups

In pan, combine cream and mushrooms. Bring to a boil, then reduce heat to a low simmer. Add ginger, soy sauce, salt and pepper. Simmer for another 3 or 4 minutes, or until the sauce is reduced to the consistency you like. Keep warm.

Note: *Use 1 cup each of your favorite stir-fry vegetables.*

Ono with Chinese Flavored Broth

Serves 4

Ono, also called wahoo, is a light white flaky fish. The hot broth is the cooking agent here. In a large bowl, the thinly sliced fish circles the center filled with the mushrooms and spinach and vegetables. Then the boiling chicken broth is ladled over all.

1 quart low-sodium chicken broth

1 pound block ono (wahoo)

1/2 cup rinsed and sliced fresh shiitake mushrooms

1/2 cup spinach leaves, julienned and stems removed

1/2 cup small diced bell pepper (any color)

1/2 cup julienned green onions

1/2 cup peeled and julienned fresh ginger

1/2 cup coarsely chopped fresh cilantro

Heat broth to a boil. Thinly slice ono (1 x 1 x 1/8-inch pieces) and place fish around bowl. Place mushrooms and spinach in bowl center. Sprinkle diced bell pepper, julienned ginger, and green onions on fish. Ladle hot broth over fish and garnish with cilantro.

GALLO *of* SONOMA
RUSSIAN RIVER VALLEY
Pinot Noir
BARREL AGED
1998

MacNut Crusted Opah

Serves 6

Delicate moonfish dressed in macadamia nuts. The egg dip allows the mac nuts to stick and the quick-fry turns them a beautiful golden brown. The Sweet and Sour Sauce secret ingredients are the fresh orange juice and the orange marmalade. The garlic, ginger, and cilantro give it a kick.

Sweet and Sour Sauce (see recipe below)

2 pounds fresh opah (moonfish), cut into 2-1/2 ounce fillets (12 pieces)

2 teaspoons salt

2 teaspoons pepper

2 cups all-purpose flour for dusting

4 eggs, beaten

2-1/2 cups finely ground macadamia nuts

1/2 cup vegetable oil for deep-frying

Season opah fillets with salt and pepper, and dust both sides of fillets with flour, shaking excess flour off. Dip opah into beaten eggs and then roll in macadamia nuts until well coated.

Heat oil in wok to 350°F. Fry opah fillets a few at a time for 4 to 5 minutes or until golden brown. Drain briefly on paper towels. Allow oil to return to 350°F. before adding new batch of fillets.

Serve MacNut Crusted Opah on individual plates or platter and pour Sweet and Sour Sauce over the top.

* Baked opah with this sauce is great, too.

Sweet and Sour Sauce

Makes 3 cups

1 cup granulated sugar

1 cup rice wine vinegar

Juice of 4 oranges (1-1/2 to 3 cups)

1-1/2 cups orange marmalade

1 teaspoon peeled and minced fresh ginger

1 teaspoon minced fresh garlic

1 teaspoon finely chopped fresh cilantro

In a saucepan, combine ingredients and cook over medium heat. Cook until the sauce reaches desired consistency. Remember to stir frequently to prevent burning. This sauce will be poured over the fish once the fish is cooked.

Mahimahi with Warm Corn Sauce & Fried Green Tomatoes

Serves 4

Mahimahi should be called the "first fish." For folks who look at fish but don't know how to cook it, this is the best to start with. Even if you overcook it a bit it will still be good. This recipe has a warm corn sauce for moistness. And real fried green tomatoes! The corn sauce takes a half hour, the fish is done in under ten minutes. Fast!

**Warm Corn Sauce
(see recipe below)**

**Fried Green Tomatoes
(see recipe on page 161)**

**4 mahimahi (dolphinfish) fillets
(6-ounces each)**

2 tablespoons kosher salt

**1/2 teaspoon coarse
ground pepper**

2 tablespoons light olive oil

Season fish with salt and pepper. Heat olive oil in a sauté pan over medium-high. Cook for 3 to 4 minutes on first side, browning well. Turn the fish and continue to cook for another 2 minutes. Drain on paper towels.

On individual plates, place approximately 3 ounces of Warm Corn Sauce in the center. Place fish on top of sauce, drizzle a little more sauce over the top. Garnish with 2 slices of fried green tomatoes.

Warm Corn Sauce

Makes 3-3/4 cups

**2 cups fresh corn kernels (canned
corn can be used)**

**1 cup chicken stock or low-sodium
chicken broth**

1 bay leaf

1 tablespoon minced fresh garlic

1/4 cup dry white wine

1/2 cup whole milk

1 teaspoon kosher salt

1/2 teaspoon coarse ground pepper

2 tablespoons sliced green onions

In a medium size saucepan, combine corn, chicken stock, bay leaf, minced garlic, and white wine. Bring mixture to a boil and reduce heat; simmer for 20 minutes. Add milk, salt, ground pepper, and green onions and continue to simmer for an additional 10 minutes.

Remove the bay leaf. Adjust seasonings if necessary. Keep warm until ready to serve.

Fried Green Tomatoes

2 large green tomatoes
1 tablespoon kosher salt
1/2 teaspoon coarse ground pepper
1 cup all-purpose flour
1 cup eggs, beaten
1 cup yellow corn meal
Peanut oil for frying

Makes 8 slices

Cut each tomato into 4 slices (3/4-inch thick). Season with salt and pepper. Place flour, beaten eggs, and cornmeal in three separate shallow bowls. Dust each tomato slice with flour, dip in whipped eggs, and drench in cornmeal. Set aside.

Warm peanut oil in a heavy-bottomed skillet. The oil should be about 1/2-inch deep. When the oil is hot, pan-fry the tomato slices for about 30 seconds on each side or until well browned. Drain on paper towels.

Island Swordfish

Cooked on a grill, this fish dish has a wonderful, Dijon mustard flavor. The homemade salsa starts with a ripe mango and a papaya. The spices, hot chili pepper and fresh lime make it perfect for the grilled fish. If your grill isn't handy, a hot skillet can create almost the same result.

Fruit Salsa (see recipe below)
4 (4-ounce) swordfish steaks (3/4-inch thick)
2 tablespoons rice vinegar
2 tablespoons Dijon mustard
1/2 cup soy sauce
3 tablespoons granulated sugar
Vegetable oil cooking spray

Garnish:

Fresh cilantro sprigs

Combine rice vinegar, Dijon mustard, soy sauce, and sugar in a small bowl and whisk until well blended. Brush vinegar mixture over steaks.

Coat grill rack with vegetable oil spray. Grill steaks over medium-hot coals for 5 minutes per side or until done (see Note). Transfer steaks to individual plates and serve with 1/4 cup Fruit Salsa. Garnish with cilantro sprigs.

Fruit Salsa

1/2 cup ripe chopped mango
1/4 cup chopped, seeded papaya
2 tablespoons finely chopped celery
1 tablespoon minced fresh cilantro
2 tablespoons fresh lime juice
1/4 cup finely chopped purple onion
1 tablespoon peeled and minced fresh ginger
1/2 tablespoon Hawaiian chili pepper, seeded and minced
1 tablespoon granulated sugar
1/4 cup edible flowers such as pansies and 1/2 cup nasturtiums (optional)

Makes about 1-1/4 cups

Combine all ingredients in a small bowl, mix well.

Note: *Swordfish also could be seared in hot skillet prepared with vegetable oil spray.*

Blackened Swordfish

Serves 4

Paul Prudhomme created a great Blackened Red Fish Magic.
Roll the fish in the magic. Get that oil smoking and cook the fish quickly.
Pour warm Soy Sauce Butter Sauce over the blackened fish
and the platter will be empty in minutes!

**Soy Sauce Butter Sauce
(see recipe below)**

**12 pieces (3-ounce each)
of kujiki (swordfish)**

**3/4 cup Paul Prudhomme's
Blackened Red Fish Magic**

2 tablespoons oil

Roll the swordfish in Blackened Red Fish Magic. In a heavy skillet, heat oil until it starts to smoke. Carefully, lower the fish into the hot oil. Cook about 3 minutes on each side, depending on the thickness of the fish. Serve with Soy Sauce Butter Sauce.

Soy Sauce Butter Sauce

Makes 2-1/3 cups

5 tablespoons soy sauce

2 tablespoons oyster sauce

1 pound butter

In a sauce pot, heat soy sauce and oyster sauce until simmering. With the heat on medium, gradually add butter while continually whisking with a wire whisk until everything has been added. Serve while warm over blackened fish.

GALLO *of* SONOMA
SONOMA COUNTY
Merlot
BARREL AGED
1997
ALC. 13 PS BY VOL.

Red Snapper with Tamarind Pineapple Sauce

Serves 2

Turn the whole snapper golden brown with a wok fry.
Cover with the tart/sweet Tamarind Sauce. Made with the tamarind pulp,
a fresh pineapple, many favorite spices and herbs, a bit of brown sugar and butter,
this sauce is like a very different tangy chutney.

**Tamarind Sauce
(see recipe below)**
1 whole snapper (1-1/2 pound)
1 cup all-purpose flour
Vegetable oil for frying

Garnish:

Wedges of fresh pineapple
**4 tablespoons chopped fresh cilantro
(optional)**

Preheat wok with oil. Dredge fish in flour, shake off excess, and fry. Turn fish over and cook until done. The snapper should be golden brown in color.

Place snapper on large oval plate and pour Tamarind Sauce over it. Serve with wedges of pineapple and chopped cilantro if desired.

Tamarind Sauce

1/2 cup tamarind pulp
1-1/2 cup water
2 tablespoons butter, melted
2 cups medium diced fresh pineapple
1 onion, medium diced
3 stalks green onions, minced
1 tomato, medium diced
1 teaspoon minced fresh garlic
1 teaspoon minced fresh cilantro
2 tablespoons brown sugar
1/2 teaspoon black pepper
1/2 teaspoon minced fresh thyme
1/4 teaspoon ground cloves
1/4 teaspoon ground allspice
1/4 teaspoon salt

Makes about 2 cups

Combine tamarind pulp and water in saucepan. Bring to a simmer, stirring frequently. Cook for 5 minutes and then drain liquid into a container for later use; discard pulp.

In a saucepan, add butter, pineapple, onions, green onions, tomato, garlic and cilantro. Sauté over medium heat for 8 to 10 minutes. Add tamarind liquid, brown sugar, black pepper, thyme, cloves, allspice, and salt to pan. Simmer for 15 minutes or until the mixture consistency is similar to chutney.

Scene IV – Shellfish

When it's showtime and I have a platter of lobster sitting out, ready to prepare, my guests, the producer and even the cameramen's mouths begin to water. Lobster really is the "King of Seafood." Jumbo shrimp run a close second. I laugh when I think that, growing up, we called lobsters "bugs!" They are still called that all over Australia.

Lobster, and other shellfish, cook quickly. They get very rubbery if they are overcooked. The shellfish flavors are light. Your seasoning can be innovative, just not overpowering.

I love to fill a bowl with scallops, clams, lobster, crab, fish and vegetables. It becomes a seafood stew or cioppino or bouillabaisse. Leaving the shells on the clams and crabs

gives that "gourmet" look to the dish. However it is served, it says one thing, "abundance." Sam's Walk into the Wok combines nearly all my favorites. Good scrubbing of shells, proper handling of crab, it all makes for a perfect dish.

I love to include the fermented black soy bean in shellfish dishes. Don't confuse this with the small, dried black bean used in Hispanic food. This is the soft black bean, almost paste, that adds sweetness and salt taste to Island dishes. Use it sparingly.

Shrimps, jumbo and other size, have un-ending possibilities of preparation. Cold and hot, shelled or not, you can sauté them, flame them, even cook them with the heads on. Just remember, the fresher the shrimp the sweeter the taste, and, the minute they turn pink they are done.

Kahuku Shrimp & Kahuku Eggplant Stir-Fry

Serves 4

*This is a fast trip through Kahuku! Hot wok.
One minute of cooking for the shrimp and sliced eggplant. One minute with
the spices. Two minutes with the sauce. Thicken a bit and
put it on the noodles. Dinner—quick!*

2 tablespoons salad oil

**8 whole Kahuku extra jumbo shrimp
(16 to 20 count), peeled and deveined**

**2 large Kahuku eggplant,
sliced into 1-inch chunks**

1 tablespoon minced fresh garlic

**1 tablespoon peeled and
minced fresh ginger**

1 teaspoon red chili pepper flakes

1 tablespoon oyster sauce

1 tablespoon soy sauce

Pinch of salt and pepper

**1 cup chicken stock or low-sodium
chicken broth**

**2 tablespoons cornstarch mixed
with 2 tablespoons water**

Heat oil in the wok over high heat.
Add shrimp and eggplant and cook
about 1 minute. Add the garlic,
ginger, chili flakes, and sauté another
minute or so. Add the oyster sauce,
soy sauce, chicken stock, salt, and
pepper. Cook about 2 minutes until
shrimp are just cooked and eggplant is
slightly soft. Stir in cornstarch mixture
and let it come to a boil.

Serve over noodles or rice and enjoy!

Shrimp Scampi with Rotelli Pasta

Serves 6

This recipe takes a bit of time and hand work. The shrimp stays "dressed" in its shell. Butterfly, coat with a butter and herb sauce and then bake with the second generation cream and stock sauce. By keeping the shell on, the baked shrimp will stand nicely, tails proudly in the air, around the cooked, sauce-drenched pasta.

2 pounds extra jumbo shrimp (16 to 20 count)

3/4 cup sweet butter, clarified

1/4 cup light olive oil

2 tablespoons minced fresh garlic

Juice from 1 lemon (about 2 tablespoons)

1/2 teaspoon dry mustard

1 tablespoon chili paste

1 teaspoon minced fresh oregano

1 teaspoon minced fresh tarragon

1 teaspoon minced fresh sweet basil

1/4 teaspoon salt

4 tablespoons minced fresh cilantro

1/2 cup chicken stock or low-sodium chicken broth

1/2 cup cream or whole milk

2 cups mixed vegetables (such as mushrooms, zucchini, and carrots)

1 pound rotelli pasta

1/3 cup freshly grated Parmesan cheese

Devein shrimp and without removing shell, butterfly them. Set aside.

Melt the butter in a large skillet. Add olive oil, garlic, lemon juice, dry mustard, chili paste, oregano, basil, tarragon, salt, and 2 tablespoons cilantro. Mix well and simmer over low heat until garlic is just blond. Remove from heat.

Take each shrimp by the tail and wipe the flesh side in the mixture so that they are thoroughly coated. After dipping, arrange shrimp next to each other, flesh side up, in a foil lined pan.

Preheat oven to 400°F. and prepare pasta according to package directions. Steam mixed vegetables or cook to your liking.

Add stock to the skillet, bring to a boil, add cream and simmer until the liquid has reduced by one-fourth. Spoon some of the sauce over each shrimp. Bake for about 15 minutes. Pasta and shrimp should be done at about the same time. Turn off oven and drain the pasta.

Fork a small mound of pasta in the center of six warm plates, leaving room around the edges for the shrimp. Remove shrimp from the oven and arrange six shrimp, with tails pointing outward, around the perimeter of the pasta. Pour remaining sauce over the shrimp and pasta and decorate with 2 tablespoons cilantro. Sprinkle the pasta with freshly grated Parmesan cheese.

Stir-Fried Shrimp and Island Asparagus

Serves 4

Shrimp cook very quickly. Just two minutes in the wok and you pull them out. Sauté the fresh asparagus and the bell peppers fast too. Then add the shrimp back into the wonderful fermented Asian black beans and the liquid. Have the rice or noodles ready, this dish in on the table in a few quick minutes.

12 whole extra jumbo shrimp (16 to 20 count), peeled and deveined

1 pound fresh asparagus, sliced into 1-inch pieces

1 tablespoon fermented black beans

2 tablespoons minced green onions

1 tablespoon minced fresh garlic

3 teaspoons peeled and minced fresh ginger

1 tablespoon soy sauce

1-1/2 teaspoons sesame oil

1 teaspoon brown sugar

2 teaspoons cornstarch plus 2 teaspoons water for thickening

1 tablespoon canola oil

1 bunch fresh spinach (1 cup)

1/2 red bell pepper, julienned

1/2 yellow bell pepper, julienned

1/2 cup chicken stock or low-sodium chicken broth

Prepare shrimp.

Wash asparagus and snap or trim off tough ends (generally where it breaks easily). Remove lower scales or peel bottom if desired. Slice into 1-inch pieces and simmer asparagus in boiling water until just tender.

Mash black beans with green onions, garlic, and ginger. Stir in soy sauce, sesame oil, and brown sugar. Set aside. Mix cornstarch and cold water to form a paste and set aside.

In a wok, heat 1 teaspoon canola oil and stir-fry shrimp for 2 minutes or until shrimp turns pink. Remove to a plate. Heat remaining oil and stir-fry asparagus, bell peppers, and spinach. Stir in black bean mixture and shrimp. Add stock and heat quickly. Add cornstarch paste a little at a time to thicken. Serve over steamed rice or noodles.

Assorted Seafood Laulau

Serves 1 laulau

Mahimahi, scallops and shrimp all become close friends in Sam's laulau. The soy-mayonnaise mixture, layered between the fish and vegetables, is rich and moist. Scallops and shrimp are added at the top. Steam for the proper time, bring out the poi and eat them.

I quart water

6 tablespoons mayonnaise

2 teaspoons soy sauce

I teaspoon chopped dill

Salt and pepper to taste

2 ti leaves

3 2-1/2 ounce pieces of fresh fish
(mahimahi or salmon are best)

4 bay scallops, rinsed and shelled

4 bay shrimp, peeled
and deveined

1/2 cup fresh spinach leaves

1/2 cup julienned carrots

1/2 cup julienned zucchini

2 rinsed and sliced fresh
shiitake mushrooms

Other assorted seafood
(optional)

In a small bowl, combine mayonnaise, soy sauce, fresh dill, salt and pepper. Mix well. Set aside.

Take 2 medium-sized ti leaves and with a sharp knife remove the ribs. Then with tip of a knife, barely tap the rib midway. Pull the rib completely off of 2 ti leaves. On 1 of the leaves, split the stem to the bottom of the leaf.

Criss-cross the 2 leaves to make the base of the laulau. Begin layering laulau with 1 piece of fish, then a dollop of mayonnaise-soy sauce mix, followed by zucchini, carrots, spinach, and a couple slices of shiitake mushrooms. Repeat this process 2 more times stacking the fish and other items. At the very top, add the bay shrimp and scallops and whatever other kind of seafood you desire. Pulling the stems up, wrap the split stems around the other 2 stems and in a knot so that a pouch is formed.

Place a steaming rack in a 4-quart pot along with 1/2 to 1-quart of water. Heat until water is at a rapid boil. Carefully place laulau in pot and cover. Steam for approximately 15 to 20 minutes or until done.

Carefully remove laulau and serve with rice or poi.

Ocean Sake Pasta

Serves 6

*This is a "pound-a" dinner. A pound of shrimp, a pound of scallops
and a pound of crab. Sauté up the pounds, give it a drink of sake and drench it
in the tomato, ginger and sake Seafood Pasta Sauce,
served over two pounds of pasta.*

Seafood Pasta Sauce (see recipe below)
2 pounds cooked linguine
1 tablespoon vegetable oil
2 teaspoons minced fresh garlic
**1 pound whole extra jumbo shrimp
(16 to 20 count), peeled and deveined**
1 pound scallops, rinsed
1 pound crabmeat,
**2 teaspoons each of salt and
white pepper**
1/2 cup sake (sweet Japanese rice wine)

Garnish:
1/2 cup chopped fresh cilantro

In a large pot, heat water and a pinch of salt to boil pasta.

Meanwhile, heat 1 tablespoon oil or enough oil to coat bottom of sauté pan over medium heat. Add garlic, sauté 30 seconds, then add all seafood. Season with salt and pepper and sauté for 2 to 3 minutes. Add sake and let liquid reduce by half.

Add Seafood Pasta Sauce and bring to a slight boil. Reduce heat and let simmer for 5 minutes.

During this time, begin cooking your pasta according to package directions. Rinse well and drain. Toss pasta with seafood sauce. Serve immediately.

Seafood Pasta Sauce

2 tablespoons olive oil
4 teaspoons minced fresh garlic
2 shallots, minced
**1 tablespoon peeled and
minced fresh ginger**
2 cups diced tomatoes
**1/2 cup sake (sweet
Japanese rice wine)**
2 tablespoons granulated sugar
2 tablespoons Asian chili sauce
1/2 teaspoon each salt and pepper

Makes about 3 cups

Combine all ingredients in a saucepan and simmer over medium heat. Stir occasionally and set aside.

Sam's Bambucha Seafood Pot Pie

Serves 4

Scallops, clams, shrimp, sweet potato and ready-made puff pastry
make this pie very easy. Do some chopping for the pie filling and the broth.
Layer in the filling, cover with the saffron-flavored broth,
and give it 30 minutes in the oven.

**Pot Pie Broth
(see recipe on page 174)**

**1/4 cup cleaned and chopped
fresh spinach**

**1/3 cup rinsed and sliced fresh
shiitake mushrooms**

**1/2 cup king crabmeat, already
removed from shell**

**4 whole extra jumbo shrimp
(16 to 20 count), peeled and
deveined**

**4 each scallops, rinsed in cold
water and shelled**

**4 each clams, rinsed in
cold water and shelled**

4 ounces fresh fish, diced

Salt and pepper to taste

**1 tablespoon chopped
green onions**

**2 tablespoons finely chopped
fresh cilantro or to taste**

**1/3 cup sweet potatoes,
cooked and chopped**

**Ready-made puff pastry
or pie dough**

2 eggs, beaten

Preheat oven to 350° F.

In a large 10-inch diameter baking dish, layer spinach, mushrooms and mixed seafood. Add salt and pepper to taste. Scatter in green onions, cilantro, and sweet potatoes. Pour in prepared broth to cover pot pie filling.

Cover dish with ready-made puff pastry or pie dough. Seal sides of dough to baking dish. Brush with eggs and bake for 30 minutes or until pie top is golden brown.

Pot Pie Broth

Vegetable oil spray
1 tablespoon minced fresh garlic
1 tablespoon peeled and grated ginger
1 cup sliced onions
1 cup sliced celery
2 cups stewed tomatoes
2 cups clam juice
1 tablespoon saffron
Salt and pepper to taste
3 tablespoons butter

Makes about 5 cups

Spray a wok with vegetable oil and heat to medium; brown garlic and ginger. Add onions, celery, and stewed tomatoes. Add clam juice and saffron and bring to a boil. Add salt and pepper to taste. Top off with butter and simmer until broth thickens.

Sautéed Clams, Shrimp, and Scallops with Black Bean Sauce

Serves 6

The black bean flavor is really taking off, like poke. At first it was just in Hawai'i. Now the word is spreading and it won't be long until it is "mainsream." This is fast! Washed seafoods take a quick sauté in a hot wok. Then the vegetables jump in, followed by the sauce ingredients. The black beans add the Asian magic.

36 fresh clams (with shells)

1/2 pound large scallops

1/2 pound whole extra jumbo shrimp (16 to 20 count)

1-1/2 tablespoons peanut oil for frying

1 cup mixed julienned vegetables

1 tablespoon minced fresh garlic

1 tablespoon peeled and grated fresh ginger

3 tablespoons dau see, washed, drained and mashed (fermented black beans)

1 tablespoon granulated sugar

3 tablespoons soy sauce

1 cup low-sodium chicken broth

1 tablespoon garlic chili sauce

Garnish:

Sliced green onion

Chopped fresh cilantro

To prepare shellfish:

First prepare clams before opening them by scrubbing them with a brush while under cold running water (any clam which remains open when tapped should be discarded). Rinse scallops in cold water and drain well on paper towels. Peel and devein shrimp.

Heat peanut oil in wok over medium-high heat. Add clams still in shells and sauté for 1 minute. Then add scallops, shrimp, and mixed vegetables and stir-fry for another minute. Add remaining ingredients and stir. Sauté until everything is well coated and clam shells open.

Garnish with green onions and chopped cilantro. Serve immediately.

GALLO *of* SONOMA
RUSSIAN RIVER VALLEY
Pinot Noir
BARREL AGED   *1998*

Seafood and Sausage in a Kakaako Créme Broth

Serves 8

Portuguese sausage isn't what you would expect to find with shrimp and clams but it works. Fresh tomatoes, two kinds of onions, a bit of butter, and some clam stock make it easy. The magic flavor — Sam's Kakaako Créme Ale Beer.

1 teaspoon vegetable oil

1 tablespoon minced fresh garlic

1 tablespoon peeled and grated fresh ginger

3 pounds whole extra jumbo shrimp (16 to 20 count), peeled and deveined

3 pounds fresh clams, rinsed and shelled

1 cup sliced sweet onions

1 cup sliced yellow onions

10 ounces Portuguese sausage, diced

3 cups clam stock

2 cups diced tomatoes

1/4 cup chopped green onions

3 tablespoons butter

1/2 cup Kakaako Créme Ale Beer (Note: this is Sam's brew but can substitute with any beer)

In a large wok, sauté garlic and ginger in medium-hot oil and quickly brown. Add shrimp and clams and stir-fry. Add sweet and yellow onions and Portuguese sausage. When sausage is medium cooked, add clam stock, tomatoes, green onions, butter, and the Kakaako Créme Ale Beer. Bring to a boil, then serve.

Spaghetti with White Clam Sauce

Serves 4

Real clams, with shells, make this dish great tasting and great looking. Instead of a plain white clam sauce, here you add carrots and zucchini for color and flavor. Wok the garlic and clams; add the broth and heavy cream. The clams open and pow—you're ready. Have your pasta prepared, the sauce cooks very quickly.

1 pound spaghetti

1/4 cup sweet butter

2 teaspoons minced fresh garlic

2 tablespoons chopped fresh cilantro

2 cans (6-1/2 ounce each) minced clams, undrained

1 dozen fresh clams

1/2 cup long julienned carrots and zucchini

1/2 teaspoon salt

1/8 teaspoon pepper

1/4 cup white wine

1/2 cup chicken stock or low-sodium chicken broth

1/4 cup heavy cream or whole milk

1/2 cup fresh grated Parmesan cheese

Garnish:

Fresh cilantro and basil, as desired

In a large pot, boil water and prepare pasta according to package directions. Drain.

Melt butter in wok. Add garlic and stir-fry until light brown. Add 2 tablespoons cilantro, minced clams, and fresh clams. Toss gently for 30 seconds. Add carrots and zucchini, salt, and pepper, and white wine. Simmer for 1 minute. Add chicken stock, heavy cream and Parmesan cheese. Simmer for another couple minutes until sauce thickens and clams open.

Garnish with cilantro and basil if desired and pour over hot spaghetti. Toss gently.

GALLO *of* SONOMA
RUSSIAN RIVER VALLEY
Chardonnay
BARREL FERMENTED
1998

Chef Elmer's Dungeness Crab Boil

Serves 4

The crab-with-shell, deveined shrimp in the shell, and mussels and clams with shells are all tied together with the other ingredients in a boiling bundle. When the well-spiced Poaching Liquid comes to a boil, in goes the bundle. Ten minutes later, out comes a dish fit for royalty.

Crab Boil Poaching Liquid (see recipe on page 180)

1/4 pound sweet potato, large dice

1/4 pound taro, large dice

4 clams

4 mussels

4 whole extra jumbo shrimp (16 to 20 count)

1 dungeness crab, quartered

1/4 pound rinsed fresh shiitake mushroom caps

1 Portuguese sausage, cut in 4 pieces

1 large piece cheesecloth

4 garlic bulbs

In a large pot, heat Crab Boil Poaching Liquid to a boil.

To prepare seafood, scrub shellfish with cold running water before opening. Remove shaggy beard from mussels before cooking. Devein shrimp, but leave shell. To clean a crab, hold the legs down with the right hand while gripping the head of the crab from underneath with the left hand. With even pressure, pull the "helmet" off the crab. Remove gills and mouth.

Rinse clean cheesecloth in water to remove lint. Lay cheesecloth flat on a table and place seafood, shiitake mushrooms, sausage, and garlic in the center of the cloth. Pull together each corner to form a bag, knotting it at the top. Place "crab boil" in boiling poaching liquid for 10 to 12 minutes.

Remove cheesecloth bag from liquid. Divide ingredients between 4 serving bowls (each person getting equal shares of seafood). Serve with melted butter.

Poaching liquid

2 gallons water
3 tablespoons Hawaiian salt
3 tablespoons cayenne pepper
1/2 cup paprika
2 lemons halved, juiced
2 large pieces of ginger, smashed
8 garlic cloves
1 tablespoon cracked black pepper
2 stalks lemon grass

Makes 2 gallons

Combine all ingredients in a large pot and boil for 10 minutes until flavors are absorbed. Reduce heat to a simmer. This poaching liquid is ready to use.

Capellini Pasta with Crab Sauce

Serves 4

Get the pasta ready! Chop tomato, some green onions, mince a bit of garlic and get everything in the pan for two minutes. Give the crab another two minutes and this crab sauce is served!

Crab Sauce (see recipe below)
I pound capellini pasta

Cook capellini according to package directions. Drain and place pasta in serving bowls and top with Crab Sauce. Enjoy!

Crab Sauce

Makes 3 Cups

I tablespoon butter
I teaspoon minced fresh garlic
1/2 cup chopped green onions
2 tomatoes, peeled, seeded, and chopped
1/2 pound crab meat, cooked, and shredded
I tablespoon fresh lemon juice
1/2 teaspoon celery salt
Cracked black pepper to taste
1/4 cup chopped fresh parsley

In a sauce pan, combine butter, garlic, and green onions. Cook about 3 to 4 minutes. Add tomatoes and simmer for 1 to 2 minutes more. Add crab meat, lemon juice, celery salt and cracked black pepper. Cook an additional 2 minutes. Add chopped parsley.

GALLO *of* SONOMA
RUSSIAN RIVER VALLEY
Chardonnay
BARREL FERMENTED   *1998*
ALC. 13.5% BY VOL.

Island-Style Lobster Boil
with Hawaiian Salt, Chili Peppers & Other Things...

Serves 4

This is a simple way to get the "King of Seafood" to the table. The Poaching Liquid is rich with the flavor of cilantro, pepper corns, carrot, celery, chili peppers, and a bit of white wine. After the "King" takes a 10-minute boil, he needs an ice water bath before being chopped into melt-in-the-mouth bite-sized pieces.

Lobster Poaching Liquid
(see recipe below)

4 Whole Kona lobsters
(about 1 pound)

In a large pot, bring Lobster Poaching Liquid to a boil. Immerse whole lobster into boiling water for approximately 10 minutes. Using tongs, carefully remove lobster from water and immediately submerge tails into a large bowl of ice water. When completely cooled, remove lobster from shell and cut lobster into small pieces.

Serve lobster with cooked carrots, onions, celery, and some of the reserved water.

Lobster Poaching Liquid

Makes 5 cups

Pinch of Hawaiian salt
1 or 2 crushed chili peppers
1 lemon, cut into quarters
1 carrot, coarsely chopped
1 celery stalk, coarsely chopped
1 onion, coarsely chopped
1 tablespoon chopped fresh cilantro
1 tablespoon cracked peppercorns
2 tablespoons white wine
3 cups water

Stir-Fried Tofu and Scallops with Mixed Greens

Serves 4

Stir-fry with an Asian look and taste. Golden fried tofu squares mix with lightly sautéed scallops and shiitake mushrooms. The mixed vegetables are cooked crisp. The bed of long rice looks exotic when the contents of the wok are poured over. No time for photos, this is quick cook and eat!

2 small packages long rice (about 2 ounces each)

1 package (20 ounces) firm tofu, cubed and deep fried

Cornstarch for dusting

2 cups vegetable oil for deep-frying

1 pound fresh scallops, rinsed and shelled

12 rinsed and sliced fresh shiitake mushrooms

8 cups mixed vegetables (such as Chinese peas, carrots, daikon, etc.)

1 tablespoon sake (sweet Japanese rice wine)

4 tablespoons soy sauce

2 tablespoons minced fresh garlic

2 tablespoons peeled and grated fresh ginger

2 teaspoons ground white pepper

2 teaspoons red hot pepper flakes

1 teaspoon salt

Cook long rice until translucent.

To fry tofu, cut into cubes and drain off any excess water. Dust in cornstarch, shaking off any excess. Pour 2 cups of oil into a medium sauce pan and heat until approximately 325°F. Deep-fry tofu until golden brown. Drain on paper towels.

In a wok, place enough oil to cover wok sides and heat to medium heat. Add scallops and shiitake mushrooms. Add mixed vegetables, sake, and remaining ingredients. Stir in tofu. Pour over long rice and serve.

* Use low-fat extra firm silken tofu in place of regular firm tofu to decrease total fat by 9 grams per serving and 80 Calories per serving.

Hawaiian Escargot Stew

Serves 4

First you simmer the escargot, then put some butter in the wok, add onions, mushrooms, and cream. The hot stew is great alone or with a friendly chunk of steak.

Vegetable oil spray

1 pound fresh Hawaiian escargot (farm-raised locally)

Water

1/8 teaspoon salt for water

4 tablespoons butter

1 tablespoon minced fresh garlic

3 tablespoons minced onion

1/4 pound rinsed and sliced fresh oyster mushrooms

1/4 pound rinsed and sliced fresh shiitake mushrooms

3 cups heavy cream

Salt to taste

Sear escargot in oiled hot deep heavy skillet. Add salted water and slowly simmer escargot for 2-1/2 hours or until tender. Chop coarsely and set aside.

Combine butter, garlic, and onion in a wok over medium heat. Cook until onion is slightly translucent. Add braised escargot and mushrooms, stir. Add cream and reduce liquid until almost gravy-like in texture.

Option: Serve hot escargot stew in a cooked pastry bowl or over your favorite steak!

* Use half and half in place of heavy cream to cut the fat by 9 grams per serving.

Sautéed Scallops with Lu'au Sauce

Serves 6

Lu'au is the name for young taro tops. The name eventually became the name of a big Hawaiian feast. In this case, the Scallops in Lu'au Sauce really is a feast. With the stems removed, you blanch the leaves. The sauce is creamy with coconut milk, butter and heavy cream. Add the lu'au leaves, simmer, plate and let the golden brown scallops float in the center.

Lu'au Sauce (see recipe below)
2 pounds fresh large scallops
2 tablespoons all-purpose flour
Salt and pepper to taste
I tablespoon salad oil

Rinse scallops in cold water and drain well on paper towels.

Combine flour with salt and pepper. Dust scallops with flour mixture. Place oil in sauté pan and heat to medium-high. Sauté scallops until evenly browned.

Ladle Lu'au Sauce onto individual plates and arrange scallops on top. Serve.

Lu'au Sauce

I cup cooked and chopped lu'au leaves (young taro leaves), or spinach leaves
1/2 cup diced onions
2 tablespoons butter
1/4 cup heavy cream
1/4 cup coconut milk
Salt and pepper to taste
I tablespoon granulated sugar
1/2 cup chicken stock or low-sodium chicken broth

Makes 2 cups

To cook lu'au leaves, remove stem from leaves, chop and then blanch into boiling water for 3 to 5 minutes. Strain in colander.

In a sauce pan, brown onions in butter over medium heat. Add heavy cream and coconut milk. Season with salt, pepper and sugar. Let simmer for 5 minutes. Add cooked lu'au leaves and chicken stock. Simmer for 15 to 20 minutes.

* For a lower fat, yet thicker sauce, substitute coconut milk with low-fat coconut milk and thicken it to desired consistency with 1 part cornstarch to 5 parts liquid.

Chinese Scallops Chili-Ginger Oil and Black Beans

Serves 4

The delicate scallop, contrasted with just the right amount of ginger and the pungent black beans, some fresh red and yellow bell pepper and dark green spinach leaves...the result is delicious and beautiful.

**Chili Ginger Oil
(see recipe on page 189)**

1 pound sea scallops

2 tablespoons peanut oil

4-inch piece fresh ginger, peeled and thinly sliced

3 tablespoons preserved black beans

1/4 cup dry sherry

1/2 large red bell pepper, julienned

1/2 large yellow bell pepper, julienned

2 cups fresh spinach leaves, rinsed and dried

Rinse scallops in cold water and drain well on paper towels. Set aside.

In a wok, heat peanut oil over medium-high heat. Add ginger and scallops. Cook for 2 minutes, stirring frequently. Add black beans, sherry, and bell peppers, and cook for 1 more minute, stirring constantly.

Remove scallops and peppers from heat and arrange on bed of fresh spinach leaves. Drizzle with Chili Ginger Oil. Serve immediately.

* In place of 2 tablespoons peanut oil, use 1 teaspoon peanut oil and a non-stick skillet to decrease total fat by 6 grams and 50 Calories per serving.

GALLO *of* SONOMA
RUSSIAN RIVER VALLEY
Chardonnay
BARREL FERMENTED   *1998*
ALC. 13.5% BY VOL.

Chili Ginger Oil

1/2 cup peanut oil

4 fresh Hawaiian chili peppers, split and chopped

4-inch piece peeled and minced fresh ginger

2 cloves fresh garlic, thinly sliced

2 tablespoons sesame oil

2 tablespoons soy sauce

Makes 3/4 cup

Heat peanut oil in a wok over medium heat. Add chili peppers, ginger and garlic. Stir constantly for 2 minutes (Be careful because the oil will sizzle). Add sesame oil and soy sauce and cook for 2 more minutes. Remove from heat, cool slightly and strain. Set aside.

* Remember each tablespoon contains about 14 grams of total fat and 125 Calories, so use sparingly.

Sea Scallops with Chanterelles and Vinaigrette

Serves 4

This takes a two-fisted "wok-doc." Sauté scallops in one while you combine the chanterelle mushrooms, onions, tomatoes, and soy sauce and stir-fry in the other. It takes a fast hand. Plate the scallops then drizzle the pre-mixed Dijon and ginger vinaigrette over the top. Make it beautiful with a dozen edible pansies.

Prepare Sea Scallops Vinaigrette (see recipe on page 192)
20 sea scallops (about 1 pound)
2 cups all-purpose flour
1/2 tablespoon sesame seeds
1 teaspoon ginger powder
1/8 teaspoon salt
1/16 teaspoon pepper
2 tablespoons vegetable oil
1 cup fresh chanterelle mushrooms slices
1/2 cup sliced Maui onion
1 tablespoon chopped scallions or green onions
1 tablespoon diced tomatoes
1 tablespoon soy sauce
2 tablespoons chicken stock or low-sodium chicken broth

Garnish:
2 tablespoons chopped cilantro
Sliced green onions
12 edible flowers (pansies or nasturtiums)

Rinse scallops in cold water and drain well on paper towels. Combine flour, sesame seeds, ginger powder, salt, and pepper. Roll scallops around in flour mixture, making sure that they are well covered. Set aside until chanterelle mixture is ready for stir-frying.

In a large sauté pan, heat 1 tablespoon oil on high and sear scallops for 2 minutes on each side. In a second skillet or wok, heat remaining 1 tablespoon oil over medium-high heat. Add chanterelles and onions and stir-fry for 3 minutes. Add scallions, tomatoes, soy sauce and chicken stock and stir-fry for another 2 minutes.

On a serving platter, place the chanterelles in the middle and 5 pieces of scallops around. Spoon over scallops some of the chanterelles cooking liquid. Drizzle with vinaigrette. Garnish with chopped cilantro, scallions and edible flowers.

Sea Scallops Vinaigrette

1 tablespoon Dijon mustard
1 tablespoon chopped ginger
2 tablespoons soy sauce
1/2 cup rice wine vinegar
1 tablespoon sesame oil
Salt and pepper to taste

Makes 3/4 cup

Blend Dijon mustard, ginger, soy sauce, rice wine vinegar, sesame oil, and salt and pepper to taste. Set aside.

The sweet flavors of Hawai'i, coconut cake and haupia, candied pineapple, bananas, papaya, guava, mango, and deep dark chocolate repeat in hundreds of different dessert recipes. People in Hawai'i must all be born with a sweet tooth. It is contagious too. You live here and in no time you are looking for a bakery. And, there is one on nearly every city block.

A great chef may not be a great pastry chef. Baking and making sweet concoctions is a science. You can't just add a bit more of this and a little more of that. I watch the young pastry chefs. They really put in time honing their skills. They know all the tricks. Like when you pick a dessert recipe, remember that climate is important. If your kitchen doesn't have air conditioning and it is a hot, humid day, you can bet that your meringue will be heavy. For anything baked, the measurements must be exact.

I love to create really outrageous dessert

extravaganzas, like combining toasted coconut, the crunch of macadamia nuts, homemade ice cream, mountains of whipped cream, and under it all a Sam's Killer Brownie. Even more than creating them, I like to see my guests enjoying them.

I also like to serve a platter of a dozen kinds of fresh fruit, sliced and all laid out beautifully. Beside that, I put a very light cottage cheese, honey lime dip. It is refreshing without being over the limit in calories and fat grams.

Island Fruits with Cottage Cheese Honey Lime Dip

Serves 6 or more

As many fresh fruits as you can layer on a platter will be delicious dipped in this blend of cottage cheese, berries, honey and fresh lime.

**Cottage Cheese Honey Lime Dip
(see recipe below)
1 platter of fresh fruit
(sliced melon, strawberries,
pineapple, etc.)**

Cottage Cheese Honey Lime Dip

Makes 6 Cups

**4 cups cottage cheese
1 teaspoon fresh lime juice
1/4 cup honey
1 cup orange juice
1/2 cup blackberries
1/2 cup blueberries
1/2 cup raspberries**

Combine all ingredients in a blender until smooth.

Tip: *This fruit platter serves as an ideal buffet for a party dessert.*

* Use a low-fat cottage cheese.

Strawberry Lychee Soup

Serves 6

Some call lychee the "fruit of the gods."
Blended with strawberries, fresh or frozen, and a scoop of french vanilla
ice cream, this dessert soup could please royalty.

1 can (14-ounces) seeded lychee with juice

4 cups frozen strawberries in syrup

1/2 quart apple cider

1/2 teaspoon freshly squeezed lime juice

6 small scoops french vanilla ice cream

Garnish:

Mint leaves (sprigs)

In a blender, combine lychees, frozen strawberries, apple cider and freshly squeezed lime juice together and pour into individual serving bowls. In the middle of each bowl, add a small scoop of french vanilla ice cream. Garnish with mint leaves. Serve immediately. This is a great dessert soup!

* Use your favorite low-fat or non-fat vanilla ice cream to top off this dessert.

Sweet Macadamia Nut Bread Pudding

Serves 8

Just like your mom made, only better. Sam's bread pudding is made with Hawaiian sweet bread, macadamia nuts and a lot of eggs. Served right out of the oven, with vanilla ice cream, it tastes like home!

8 eggs

2 cups granulated sugar

4 cups milk

1 teaspoon cinnamon

2 teaspoons pure vanilla extract

1/4 cup chopped macadamia nuts

1 large loaf Hawaiian sweet bread, cut or torn into small pieces

8 scoops vanilla ice cream

In a large mixing bowl, whisk together eggs and sugar. Add milk, cinnamon, and vanilla. Mix in chopped macadamia nuts and bread and soak for half an hour. Scoop into individual greased muffin holders and bake in water bath at 300°F. for 40 minutes.

Serve bread pudding warm with ice cream.

* Use non-fat milk in place of whole milk to lower fat 4 grams per serving and top with a low-fat or non-fat vanilla ice cream to lower the fat and calories more.

Okinawan Doughnuts with a Taro Twist (Poi Andagi)

Makes about 48 Doughnuts

They will look traditional on the outside. Inside the secret ingredient (poi) will give them a slightly purple cast, and a wonderful flavor. A sugar dust is a must.

1 pound poi
2 eggs
1/2 cup granulated sugar
1 tablespoon vanilla
1-1/2 cups water
2 -1/2 cups all-purpose flour
2 -1/2 teaspoons baking powder
Vegetable oil for deep-frying

Garnish:

Powdered sugar (optional)

Preheat oil in a deep heavy kettle or wok to 350 to 370°F.

Beat poi and eggs, add sugar slowly. Once blended, stir in vanilla and water .

In another bowl, sift together flour and baking powder and then stir into poi mixture until well blended.

Scoop balls of dough (about 1 tablespoon) into hot oil. Deep-fry until golden brown. Drain on paper towels.

If desired, sprinkle top with powdered sugar.

Cookie "Poke"

It's been said that all the calories run out of cookies when they are broken. If that's true, then this is a low-cal dessert. Sam's special, double delicious Chocolate Chip, Sugar Sable and Double Chocolate Chip cookies, broken, are tossed with other wondrous treats for a double-sweet "poke" treat.

Sugar Sable Cookies
(see recipe below)
Double Chocolate Chip Cookies
(see recipe on page 200)
Chocolate Chip Cookies
(see recipe on page 200)
I cup toasted coconut flakes
I cup whole macadamia nuts
I cup chocolate chips
I pound M&M candies
(about 2 cups)

In a large bowl, mix three types of cookies. Sprinkle coconut flakes, macadamia nuts, chocolate chips, and M&M candies over cookies. Toss and serve.

Any 3 of your favorite cookie recipes can be used in place of the following recipes.

Sugar Sable Cookies

Makes about 36 cookies

I cup butter
I cup powdered sugar
I egg yolk
2-1/4 cups all-purpose flour, sifted
1/2 teaspoon salt

Preheat oven to 350°F.

In a bowl, cream butter and sugar until light and fluffy. Stir in egg yolk. Add flour and salt into the creamed mixture, mix until combined. Chill dough for one hour.

Form dough into teaspoon-size balls and place on an ungreased cookie sheet. Bake for 10 to 12 minutes, remove and cool for 5 minutes on a plate.

Double Chocolate Chip Cookies

Makes about 36 cookies

1-1/4 cup butter
2 cups granulated sugar
2 eggs
1 teaspoon pure vanilla extract
2 cups all-purpose flour, sifted
1-1/4 cups cocoa powder
1 teaspoon baking soda
2 cups semi-sweet chocolate chips

Preheat oven to 350°F.

In a bowl, cream butter and sugar until light and fluffy. Add eggs and vanilla extract until just combined.

In a separate bowl, sift together flour, cocoa powder and baking soda. Add dry ingredients to creamed mixture. Stir in chocolate chips. Mix until combined. Chill dough for one hour.

Scoop by teaspoonful onto ungreased cookie sheet and bake for 8 to 10 minutes. Cool for 5 minutes on a plate.

Chocolate Chip Cookies

Makes about 36 cookies

1 cup butter
1 cup granulated sugar
1/2 cup brown sugar
1 teaspoon pure vanilla extract
1 teaspoon heavy cream
1 egg
2-1/4 cups all-purpose flour, sifted
1/4 teaspoon baking soda
2 cups semi-sweet chocolate chips

Preheat oven to 350°F.

Cream butter, sugar, and brown sugar in a bowl until light and fluffy. Add vanilla extract, heavy cream, and egg until just combined. Mix flour and baking soda. Add in chocolate chips until combined.

Chill dough for one hour. Scoop into small 1 teaspoon size balls and place on an ungreased cookie sheet. Bake for 10 to 12 minutes. Cool for 5 minutes on a plate.

Sam's Big Island Brownies

Serves 12

*Kona coffee, freeze-dried, is the secret ingredient here.
Everything else blends into a familiar, favorite brownie taste. Cover cooled
brownies with vanilla ice cream and Homemade Hot Fudge Sauce.
Leftovers are unlikely, but the sauce keeps well refrigerated.*

**Homemade Hot Fudge Sauce
(see recipe below)**
1-1/2 blocks of butter
1-1/2 cups granulated sugar
1/4 cup water
**2 (16 ounce) packages semi-sweet
chocolate chips**
4 eggs
2 teaspoons vanilla
1-2/3 cups all-purpose flour
1/2 teaspoon salt
1/2 teaspoon baking soda
1/4 cup freeze-dried Kona coffee
1 cup macadamia nuts
2 quarts vanilla ice cream

Preheat oven to 300°F.

In a large saucepan, bring butter, sugar, and water to a boil. Remove from heat and stir in 1 package (16 oz) of chocolate chips. Mix until smooth.

In a bowl, whisk together eggs and vanilla. Pour in chocolate-butter mixture and whisk until combined.

In a separate bowl, sift together flour, baking soda, and salt. Stir dry ingredients into chocolate mixture. Add freeze dried coffee, remaining chocolate chips, and macadamia nuts.

Pour into a greased 9 x 13-inch pan. Spread mixture evenly. Bake for 35 to 45 minutes. Cool brownies for 2 hours. Cut into squares and top off with vanilla ice cream and hot fudge sauce.

Homemade Hot Fudge Sauce

1/4 cup granulated sugar
3/4 cup unsweetened cocoa powder
1/2 cup light corn syrup
1/2 cup plus 2 tablespoons water
**1 package (16 ounce) semi-sweet
chocolate chips**

Makes about 3-1/2 cups

In a medium saucepan, whisk together sugar, cocoa powder, corn syrup, and water. Bring to a boil, reduce heat, and simmer for 2 minutes, stirring constantly. Remove from heat. Stir in chocolate chips and mix until the chocolate has melted. Serve immediately over ice cream. Store leftovers in the refrigerator. Re-heat fudge sauce over low heat to soften.

Macadamia Nut Pie | *Serves 8*

*There is nothing like the taste of a pie shell filled to the brim
with macadamia nuts, baked until golden and then chilled, cut and served with
whipped cream. No matter what you had for dinner, you can't turn this one down.*

3 eggs

2/3 cup granulated sugar

1 cup light corn syrup

**1-1/2 to 2 cups chopped
macadamia nuts**

2 tablespoons melted butter

1 teaspoon vanilla

1 unbaked 9-inch pie shell

Preheat oven at 325°F.

Beat eggs with sugar and corn syrup and stir in the macadamia nuts. Add butter and vanilla and blend well.

Pour mixture into pie shell. Bake for 50 minutes or until the crust is golden and the center is somewhat set. Test this by shaking the pie gently. Let cool and chill.

Banana Poi—Tahitian-Style with Haupia Ice Cream

Serves 4

This isn't two finger poi. It is fork poi, baked from bananas. Topped with Haupia ice cream and sugar dusted won ton chips and swirls of coconut syrup, it is really 'onolicious.

6 ripe bananas
2 tablespoons granulated sugar
1/4 cup lemon juice
1/2 cup water
2 tablespoons cornstarch
1 tablespoon vanilla
1/2 cup water
Vegetable oil spray
4 scoops of Haupia or coconut ice cream
1/2 cup coconut syrup
1 cup won ton chips dusted with powdered sugar

Garnish:
4 mint leaf sprigs

Preheat oven to 350°F.

In a medium saucepan, mash bananas, then add sugar, lemon juice, and water. Simmer for 30 minutes. Pour banana mixture into a blender or use a hand blender to puree.

In a small bowl, mix water and cornstarch together. Add vanilla and cornstarch mixture to banana puree and blend well.

Grease an 8 x 8- inch baking pan with vegetable oil spray. Pour banana mixture into baking pan and cover baking pan with aluminum foil. Bake for 30 to 45 minutes. Halfway through the baking process remove the aluminum foil. Remove from oven and cool for 4 to 5 hours in refrigerator.

Cut baked banana poi into 4 pieces and place into individual large bowls. Serve with haupia ice cream. Drizzle with coconut syrup and sprinkle with won ton chips dusted with powdered sugar. Garnish with mint leaves.

Sam's Killer Candy Brownies

Makes 4 Big Brownies

This basic brownie, with a bit of candy added in,
is a base for unlimited types of ice cream, fruits, and sorbets.
Or, you can just bake and EAT!

I cup melted butter
I cup brown sugar
I cup granulated sugar
4 eggs
I teaspoon vanilla
1-1/2 cups all-purpose flour
1/2 cup cocoa powder
I teaspoon baking powder
1/2 teaspoon salt
I tablespoon butter
I cup chocolate chips or candy

Preheat oven to 350°F.

In a large mixing bowl, beat melted butter, brown sugar, and granulated sugar together. Add in eggs and vanilla.

In a separate bowl, sift the dry ingredients and add to the creamed mixture. Mix until combined well.

Grease 8 x 8-inch pan with butter. Pour the brownie batter into pan and sprinkle chocolate chips or candy of your choice on top. Bake for 30 minutes. Cool on wire rack. Slice when cool.

* Cut brownies into 16 servings and serve with fresh chilled fruit like seedless grapes.

Lilikoi Chiffon Cream Pie

Serves 8

Fresh lilikoi juice is a must for this recipe. That makes it only more 'onolicious, since the lilikoi season isn't long. The fluffy egg whites keep it light; the whipped cream makes it almost sinful. Enjoy!

I tablespoon unflavored gelatin

1/4 cup cold water

4 eggs, separated

I cup granulated sugar

1/2 teaspoon salt

1/2 cup fresh lilikoi juice (passion fruit, see **Note**)

I teaspoon grated lemon rind

I 9-inch prebaked pie shell

1/2 cup cream, whipped

enough toasted shredded coconut to sprinkle on top

Soften the gelatin in the water.

Beat in the egg yolk until thick and add 1/2 cup of the sugar, the salt, and the lilikoi juice. Mix well.

Over a low heat, stir until the mixture is thickened, about 10 minutes. Add gelatin mixture and stir until the gelatin is dissolved. Remove from heat. Add lemon rind and cool until slightly congealed.

Beat egg whites with remaining 1/2 cup of sugar until stiff. Fold into gelatin mixture and pour into a cooled, baked pie shell and chill until firm. Top with whipped cream and sprinkles of toasted coconut.

*****Note:** This recipe requires fresh yellow lilikoi juice.*

Banana Brownie Splits

Serves 4

Build yourself an "industrial strength" delight. The foundation is a Killer Candy Brownie. The bricks are bananas. The mortar is vanilla ice cream and an assortment of fruits, candy, and other goodies of your choice. A simple cherry tops the whipped cream!

Sam's Killer Candy Brownie (see recipe on page 205)

2 fresh bananas, sliced in half lengthwise

4 scoops of vanilla ice cream

1 cup diced fresh mango

8 fresh raspberries

2 teaspoons li hing mui powder

16 gummy bears

1/2 cup chocolate chips

1 candy bar of your choice, broken into pieces

1 cup whipped heavy cream

4 maraschino cherries

Cut brownie into four pieces (about 4 x 4-inches). Place brownies in the bottom of 4 large bowls. Start building your split with banana slices followed by a scoop of vanilla ice cream. Continue to build splits by sprinkling a fourth of the remaining ingredients over each split. Top with whipped cream and cherries.

* Decrease the size of the brownies to half and use your favorite low-fat or non-fat vanilla ice cream.

Tropical Fruit Punch

Serves 4

*It is the Li hing mui that peps this up. Toss it all in the blender,
but save the blueberries, raspberries, and pineapple to float inside for color and fun.*

1 tablespoon Li hing mui powder

1 cup of ice cubes

1 orange, peeled and cut
into segments

1 cup sliced fresh papaya

2 strawberries

1 cup diced mango

1 small banana

1 cup fresh fruit juice
(such as orange juice)

8 blueberries

8 raspberries

1 cup diced pineapple

Purée all ingredients together in a blender except the blueberries, raspberries, and pineapple. Blend till smooth. Fold in the remaining fruit and pour into chilled glasses. Enjoy on a nice summer day!

Local Mocha

This one is not for the kids! Blend everything.
Creatively squirt some extra Hershey's chocolate syrup around the tall glass
then pour in the drink. Enjoy your brown and white "masterpiece."

2-4 cups ice
1-1/2 ounces Kahlua
1-1/2 ounces cocoa rum
3 ounces pineapple juice
1 ounce Kahluacino
1 ounce half & half
1-1/2 ounces coconut syrup
1 ounce Hershey's chocolate syrup

In a blender, combine ice and all the ingredients and puree until creamy smooth. Pour into very tall chilled glasses. Serve and enjoy!

Kids Can Cook "Edible" Fishbowl

Serves 20 to 32

Start with a clean (maybe even new) aquarium bowl. The bottom of the ocean is covered with (grape) stones. The blue (jello) ocean is filled with (gummy) fish. Looks great on the table. Get creative and add some whipped cream foam to the edge of the ocean waves when you serve it. Maybe even a sugar cookie "beach" on the side.

1 glass aquarium, well cleaned

6 packages (3-ounces each) blueberry jello

4 cups seedless white grapes, stems removed

Gummy fish (How many fish is strictly up to you and your aquarium size)

All proportions are up to you, but here are some suggestions.

Place grapes in bottom of small cleaned aquarium or a large glass bowl. Make jello according to package and pour into aquarium or bowl. When halfway set, sink gummy fish into jello and let firm.

This is a treat that even the adults will love.

We'll Be Right Back

‘ahi (yellowfin tuna); use fresh blackfin or bluefin tuna

aku (skipjack tuna); use any tuna

balsamic vinegar; use sherry vinegar

bamboo shoots; use bottled hearts of palm

basmati rice; use long grain white rice

billfish; use broadbill swordfish, Pacific blue marlin, black marlin, sailfish, striped marlin

Cajun spice; use a mixture of ground garlic, onions, chili peppers, black pepper, mustard, and celery.

capellini pasta; use vermicelli or angel hair pasta.

cayenne pepper; use any ground hot chili pepper

chanterelle mushrooms; use porcini or fresh button mushrooms

char siu; use pork marinated with sugar, salt, and hoisin sauce

cilantro (Chinese parsley); use parsley

coconut milk (thick); use 1 cup heavy cream with one teaspoon coconut flavoring

coconut milk (thin); use 1 cup whole milk beaten with 1 teaspoon coconut flavoring

cornstarch for thickening; use all-purpose flour up to 2 to 3 tablespoons

cranberries, fresh; use dried unsweetened cranberries (reconstituted)

crème fraîche (fresh creme); use 1/2 sour cream and 1/2 heavy cream

Creole mustard; use brown mustard and horseradish

daikon; use radish

edible flowers; use bachelor buttons, marigolds, nasturtiums, pansies, rose petals, or snap dragons

escargot; use any type of snail

fennel bulb; use base of celery and small amount of sweet anise

fish sauce; use 1 part soy sauce plus four parts mashed anchovies

Substitute This

fishcake; use mild-flavored white flesh fish, such as cod

furikake; use ground sesame seeds and finely chopped nori seaweed sheets

garlic cloves (1); use 1 teaspoon chopped garlic or 1/8 teaspoon garlic powder

ginger (fresh grated); go to an Asian market (powdered ginger is not a good substitute)

goat cheese; use jack or full-fat mozzarella cheese

gobo (burdock); use parsnips

Granny Smith apple; use any tart apple such as Gravenstein

Hawaiian sweet bread; use any sweet soft light bread

Hawaiian salt; use coarse sea salt

hoisin sauce; use puréed plum baby food mixed with soy sauce, garlic, and chili peppers

jicama; use water chestnuts

kabocha squash; use butter nut squash

Kahluacino; use cappuccino mixed with Kahlua

kai choy (mustard greens); use collard greens

kajiki (Pacific blue marlin); use any billfish

kalikali (kalekale); use any pink or red snapper such as ‘opakapaka

konnyaku; use firm silken tofu

kosher salt; use coarse grain sea salt

lemon grass; use lemon zest

li hing mui; use a mixture of ground dried plum or other fruit, sugar, salt, aspartame, and sometimes licorice

light olive oil; use canola oil

lu‘au leaves; use spinach leaves

lup cheung (Chinese sausage); use high fat pork sausage

lychee (fresh); use canned (in water) or peeled seedless grapes mahimahi (dolphinfish); use drum, halibut, cod, seabass, or wahoo

mango; use sweet ripe nectarine with a little lemon juice

Maui onion; use Bermuda, Vidalia, Ewa, red, or other sweet onion

mirin; use sweet sherry or sweet vermouth

miso; use condensed chicken broth blended with a small amount of tofu

mung bean thread (long rice); use any transparent noodle such as cellophane or try spaghetti squash strands

nasturtiums; see edible flowers

ogo seaweed; use finely julienned crisp cucumber plus bits of dried nori seaweed or try rinsed sweet or dill pickle

onaga (ruby red snapper); use use any pink or red snapper, such as 'opakapaka

ono (wahoo); use mahimahi, halibut, cod, kingfish, or swordfish

opah (moonfish); use monchong, amberjack, jack crevalle, or trevally

oyster mushrooms; use button mushrooms

panko; use finely ground dry bread crumbs

pansy; see edible flowers

papaya; chrensaw melon will give similar color and texture but not the same flavor

poha (Cape gooseberrry, ground cherry); use slightly sweetened tomatillos

poi; use unseasoned mashed potatoes thinned to a thick batter consistency

Portugese sausage; use mild-to-hot spicy garlic-flavored pork sausage

Portugese sweet bread; use any sweet soft light bread

prawns; use shrimp

preserved black beans; use highly salted cooked black beans

pumpkin; use acorn or butternut squash

red snapper; use any snapper or cod, haddock, or halibut

red leaf lettuce; use any leaf lettuce

red bell peppers; use any bell peppers

red oak lettuce; use any leaf lettuce

red chili pepper flakes; use finely chopped seeded red chili peppers

rice wine vinegar; use a slightly sweetened light-colored vinegar

rotelle; use wheel shaped pasta or other pasta that will capture the sauce

saffron (1/8 teaspoon); use 1/2 to 1 teaspoon turmeric

sake; use very dry sherry or vermouth

scallions; use green onions

seedless white grapes; use any seedless grape

sesame seeds; use finely chopped toasted almonds

shiitake mushrooms (fresh); use rehydrated dry shiitake or other meaty-fleshed mushroom such as portobello mushroom

snappers; use other snappers (onaga, ehu, gindai, kalekale, 'opakapaka, uku) or cod, sea bass, ocean perch, rock cod, rock fish, and whiting

snow peas; use sugar snap peas

somen noodle; use vermicelli

soy sauce; use 3 parts Worcestershire sauce to 1 part water

squid; use octopus

swordfish; see billfish or tuna

tamarind; use chopped prunes or apricots and lemon juice

taro root; use any firm fleshed potato, such as red potatoes or new potatoes

teriyaki sauce; use mixutre of soy sauce, sake or sherry, sugar, and ginger

ti leaves; use aluminum foil

wasabi (prepared); use bottled prepared horseradish with a drop of green food coloring

wasabi (powdered); use hot dry mustard

watercress; use arugula

white pepper; use black pepper

won bok; use savoy cabbage or other green cabbage

zucchini blossoms; see edible flowers

Measures and Weights

1 pinch = 1/16 to 1/8 teaspoon

3 teaspoons = 1 tablespoon

1 tablespoon = 14.8 milliliters (American)

1 tablespoon = 15 milliliters (British)

4 tablespoons = 1/4 cup

5-1/3 tablspoons = 1/3 cup

8 tablespoons = 1/2 cup

16 tablespoons = 1 cup

2 cups = 1 pint

4 cups = 1 quart

2 pints = 1 quart

1.06 quarts = 1 liter

4 quarts = 1 gallon

1 fluid ounce = 2 tablespoons = 29.6 milliliters

8 fluid ounces = 1 cup

1 cup = 235.6 milliliters (American)

1 cup = 250 milliliters (British)

1 ounce = 28.35 grams

16 ounces = 1 pound

1 pound = 454 grams

2.2 pounds = 1 kilogram

Volume versus Weight Measures

1 cup = 8 fluid ounces

1 cup may or may not weigh 8 ounces (227 grams) because of the different densities of foods.

For example:

1 cup of popped popcorn equals 8 fluid ounces but only 1/3 ounce in weight (8 to 11 grams)

1 cup chopped onion equals 8 fluid ounces but only 5-1/2 ounces in weight (155 grams)

1 cup of water equals 8 fluid ounces and about 8.3 ounces in weight (236 grams)

1 cup of tomato paste equals 8 fluid ounces but 9.2 ounces in weight (262 grams)

Stay Tuned

Recipe	Wine Recommendation
Asian-Style Poke	Gallo of Sonoma Pinot Noir
Assorted Seafood Laulau	Gallo of Sonoma Chardonnay
Baked Citrus Crusted Onaga	Gallo of Sonoma Chardonnay
Baked Luau Oysters	Gallo of Sonoma Chardonnay
BBQ Pork Tenderloin with Garlic Sauce	Gallo of Sonoma Merlot
Bean Sprout Salad	Gallo of Sonoma Chardonnay
Beef Stir-Fry	Gallo of Sonoma Zinfandel
Beef Sukiyaki	Gallo of Sonoma Merlot
Blackened Swordfish	Gallo of Sonoma Merlot
Braised Chicken	Gallo of Sonoma Pinot Noir
Breaded Oysters with Wasabi Cocktail Sauce	Gallo of Sonoma Chardonnay
Capellini Pasta with Crab Sauce	Gallo of Sonoma Chardonnay
Chef Elmer's Dungeness Crab Boil	Gallo of Sonoma Zinfandel
Chinese Scallops Chili-Ginger Oil and Black Beans	Gallo of Sonoma Chardonnay
Chicken Adobo with Sweet Potatoes	Gallo of Sonoma Merlot
Chicken and Coconut Milk	Gallo of Sonoma Chardonnay
Chicken and Egg on Rice Oyako Donburi	Gallo of Sonoma Chardonnay
Chicken and Mahimahi Laulau	Gallo of Sonoma Pinot Noir
Chicken Chili	Gallo of Sonoma Merlot
Chicken Marinara	Gallo of Sonoma Zinfandel
Chicken Salad Chinese Style with "dabest" Sauce	Gallo of Sonoma Pinot Noir

Recipe	Wine Recommendation
Chicken Sunshine Salad	Gallo of Sonoma Chardonnay
Chicken with Black Beans	Gallo of Sonoma Merlot
Chicken with Papaya and Pineapple Salad	Gallo of Sonoma Chardonnay
Cinnamon Chicken	Gallo of Sonoma Chardonnay
Cold Poached Lobster Salad	Gallo of Sonoma Pinot Noir
Corn Battered Shrimp with Tartar Sauce	Gallo of Sonoma Chardonnay
Crab Rangoon	Gallo of Sonoma Chardonnay
Crackling Duck with Vegetables	Gallo of Sonoma Cabernet Savignon
Crispy Scallop Salad	Gallo of Sonoma Chardonnay
Curried Citrus Chicken Papaya	Gallo of Sonoma Chardonnay
Drunken Shrimp	Gallo of Sonoma Chardonnay
Dungeness Crab Salad	Gallo of Sonoma Chardonnay
Fiery Chinese Beef	Gallo of Sonoma Zinfandel
Fresh Island Sautéed Spinach with Garlic	Gallo of Sonoma Chardonnay
Hana Hou Poke 7th Annual Sam Choy Poke Festival	Gallo of Sonoma Pinot Noir
Hawaiian Escargot Stew	Gallo of Sonoma Merlot
Hibachi Tofu	Gallo of Sonoma Chardonnay
Island-Style Lobster Boil with Hawaiian Salt, Chili Peppers, & Other Things…	Gallo of Sonoma Pinot Noir
Island Swordfish	Gallo of Sonoma Chardonnay
Island-Style Seafood Salad	Gallo of Sonoma Chardonnay
Jamaican Roasted pumpkin	Gallo of Sonoma Pinot Noir
Kahuku Shrimp & Kahuku Eggplant Stir-Fry	Gallo of Sonoma Zinfandel
Kalbi Ribs	Gallo of Sonoma Cabernet Sauvignon
Kalua-Style Turkey	Gallo of Sonoma Merlot
Lobster Crab Dip for Asparagus	Gallo of Sonoma Chardonnay

Recipe	Wine Recommendation
Louisiana-Style Bar-B-Que "Sam's Walk into the Wok"	Gallo of Sonoma Pinot Noir
MacNut Crusted Opah	Gallo of Sonoma Chardonnay
Mahimahi Lemon Pepper Salad	Gallo of Sonoma Chardonnay
Mahimahi with Warm Corn Sauce & Fried Green Tomatoes	Gallo of Sonoma Chardonnay
Mango Spiced Chicken	Gallo of Sonoma Chardonnay
Moloka'i Shrimp Spinach Salad	Gallo of Sonoma Chardonnay
Ono with Chinese Flavored Broth	Gallo of Sonoma Pinot Noir
Oven-Roasted Dungeness Crab with Garlic Butter	Gallo of Sonoma Pinot Noir
Oyster Poor Boy	Gallo of Sonoma Chardonnay
Pan-Fried Mullet	Gallo of Sonoma Pinot Noir
Papaya, Mint & Coconut Soup	Gallo of Sonoma Chardonnay
Pesto Brie Wheel	Gallo of Sonoma Chardonnay
Philadelphia Fish and Company's Award-Winning Crab Cakes with Curry Aioli	Gallo of Sonoma Chardonnay
Poi Stew	Gallo of Sonoma Zinfandel
Portuguese Sausage Corn Soup	Gallo of Sonoma Zinfandel
Prime Rib Roast	Gallo of Sonoma Cabernet Sauvignon
Red Snapper with Tamarind Pineapple Sauce	Gallo of Sonoma Chardonnay
Roast Leg of Lamb, Portuguese Sausage Sweet Bread Stuffing, Green Beans, and Garlic-Jalapeño Mint Jam	Gallo of Sonoma Cabernet Sauvignon
Roast Pork Loin with Goat Cheese Water Chestnut Filling	Gallo of Sonoma Pinot Noir
Roasted Sausages and Peppers	Gallo of Sonoma Zinfandel
Salmon Spread	Gallo of Sonoma Pinot Noir
Sam Choy's Big Aloha Fried Poke Wrap	Gallo of Sonoma Pinot Noir
Sam-Style Poke	Gallo of Sonoma Pinot Noir
Sam's Bambucha Seafood Pot Pie	Gallo of Sonoma Chardonnay
Sauté of Fennel, Shiitake Mushrooms and Pumpkin	Gallo of Sonoma Chardonnay

Recipe	Wine Recommendation
Sautéed Clams, Shrimp, and Scallops with Black Bean Sauce	Gallo of Sonoma Pinot Noir
Sautéed Prawns with Pickled Ginger	Gallo of Sonoma Chardonnay
Sautéed Scallops with Lu'au Sauce	Gallo of Sonoma Chardonnay
Sea Scallops with Chanterelles and Vinaigrette	Gallo of Sonoma Chardonnay
Seafood and Sausage in a Kakaako Créme Broth	Gallo of Sonoma Chardonnay
Seafood Burger	Gallo of Sonoma Chardonnay
Seafood Salad	Gallo of Sonoma Chardonnay
Sesame Crusted 'Ahi with Vegetable Trio with Chinese Vinaigrette and Curry Oil	Gallo of Sonoma Pinot Noir
Shang Hai Chicken	Gallo of Sonoma Zinfandel
Shiitake Mushroom Rice with Shredded Chicken Stir-Fry and Fresh Spinach	Gallo of Sonoma Chardonnay
Shrimp Scampi with Rotelli Pasta	Gallo of Sonoma Chardonnay
Somen Noodles with Julienne Vegetables	Gallo of Sonoma Chardonnay
South Pacific Coconut Rice with Sautéed Pork Loin	Gallo of Sonoma Pinot Noir
Spaghetti with White Clam Sauce	Gallo of Sonoma Chardonnay
Spicy Eggplant with Chicken	Gallo of Sonoma Pinot Noir
Spicy Squid Salad	Gallo of Sonoma Chardonnay
Steamed 'Opakapaka with Pink Pickled Ginger and Red Onion	Gallo of Sonoma Chardonnay
Steamed Clams with Chili and Ginger Pesto Butter	Gallo of Sonoma Chardonnay
Stir-Fried Shrimp and Island Asparagus	Gallo of Sonoma Chardonnay
Stir-Fried Tofu and Scallops with Mixed Greens	Gallo of Sonoma Pinot Noir
Stir-Fry Pepper Beef	Gallo of Sonoma Cabernet Sauvignon
Stir-fry Chicken with Fried Noodles	Gallo of Sonoma Merlot
Stuffed Eggplant	Gallo of Sonoma Chardonnay
Sweet Chili Chicken	Gallo of Sonoma Merlot

Recipe	Wine Recommendation
Tahitian Crabmeat Soup	Gallo of Sonoma Chardonnay
Teriyaki Lamb Chops with Dijon Mustard Crust	Gallo of Sonoma Cabernet Sauvignon
Teriyaki Roll-Ups	Gallo of Sonoma Merlot
Teriyaki Tofu Bean Salad	Gallo of Sonoma Zinfandel
Thai-Style Shrimp Rolls	Gallo of Sonoma Chardonnay
Winter Pumpkin Soup	Gallo of Sonoma Chardonnay

Thank You For Joining Us

'Ahi—Hawaiian name for yellowfin or bigeye tuna. Also called shibi in Japanese.

'Alaea salt—Hawaiian name for a coarse sea salt which is colored with an orange-red colored earth.

Aku—Hawaiian word for skipjack or bonito tuna. This fish is often eaten raw as an appetizer.

Al dente—Italian phrase meaning to cook foods such as pasta and vegetables to the point that they still offer a slight resistance to the bite.

Amazu shoga—Japanese word for a finely sliced beige or pink sweet pickled ginger.

Asian chili sauce—these sauces are composed of chili peppers, vinegar, salt, and sugar and range from sweet and mild to very hot and spicy.

Balsamic vinegar—a vinegar made from a white grape juice and aged in wooden barrels for a period of years. It has a very dark color and a special soft flavor that is picked up from the wood of the barrels.

Bamboo shoots—cream colored, cone shaped young shoots of the bamboo plant. Canned shoots are fine to use.

Basil—fresh or dried herb available in a variety of types including common sweet basil, opal basil, and Thai basil. These varieties can be used interchangeably.

Basmati rice—a long-grain nut-flavored rice, originated from the Himalayas.

Bay scallops-see SCALLOPS.

Bean sprouts—usually refers to sprouted mung beans, however soy beans, lentils, and sometimes other beans are used in sprouted form. Generally consumed raw or lightly stir-fried.

Bean thread noodles—a thin, clear noodle made from the starch of the mung bean. These relatively flavorless noodles soak up the flavors of other ingredients in a dish. They are also called cellophane noodles.

Black beans—these small black beans have a cream-colored sweet flesh. They are also called turtle beans and should not be confused with the salty FERMENTED BLACK BEANS.

Black goma—See SESAME SEEDS.

Bok choy —also known as pak choy or Chinese white cabbage. It has dark green leaves and long white stems.

Bonito flakes—dried tuna shavings, an important part of the stock DASHI.

Cajun spice—a mixture of spices that most commonly includes: garlic, onions, chili peppers, black pepper, mustard, and celery.

Capellini pasta—thin pasta strands slightly thicker than angel hair pasta.

Capers—pickled small flower buds of a bush native to the Mediterranean. They are added to dishes or sauces for their unique pungent salty flavor.

Chanterelle mushroom—a trumpet-shaped mushroom with a delicate fruity flavor and chewy texture. Overcooking causes the mushrooms to become tough.

Char siu—Cantonese-style marinated pork which is barbecued or roasted. It has a red color and a sweet and spicy flavor.

Chicken stock—this stock, like most, are typically made without the addition of salt. Therefore, when substituting with a canned stock or broth, the low-salt or low-sodium versions should always be used.

Chili oil—vegetable oil flavored with hot chili peppers. This can be purchased in Asian markets and should be kept refrigerated once opened.

Chili paste—composition of pastes vary, but generally include: hot red chilies, vinegar, salt, and possibly garlic.

Chop suey vegetables—a mixture of chopped vegetables, generally consisting of mushrooms, bean sprouts, onions, celery, bamboo shoots, and waterchestnuts.

Chow mein noodles—Chinese noodles generally made from wheat flour and eggs; sold dried or fresh.

Cilantro—leaves of the coriander plant. Also known as Chinese parsley.

Clarified butter—golden liquid which is separated from unsalted butter when heated. It can be used for cooking at higher temperatures due to its higher smoke point.

Coconut—the fruit or nut of the coconut palm. Most commonly available as the meat of the mature nut in shredded, flaked, and sweetened forms.

Coconut milk—the liquid extracted by squeezing the grated meat of a coconut; most often found in canned and frozen forms.

Coconut syrup—a syrup made from coconut milk and sugar.

Creole mustard—hot spicy brown mustard with a hint of horseradish.

Creole seasoning—a full-flavored seasoning that typically contains green peppers, onions, and celery along with file powder made from the leaves of the sassafras tree.

Daikon—a large Asian radish, usually white in color; it is used shredded raw for salads and garnishes or cooked similar to turnips in soups and stir-fry. Flavor ranges from mild to spicy hot.

Dashi—Japanese word for a basic soup stock made from vegetables and dried fish (bonito tuna) flakes, and kombu (kelp) and water.

Dashi-no-moto—Japanese word for instant powdered dashi, similar to powdered bouillon.

Dau see—see FERMENTED BLACK BEANS

Dijon mustard—a mild to hot prepared mustard originally from Dijon, France.

Dolphinfish—see MAHIMAHI.

Dungeness crab—a large, meaty crab that ranges from one to four pounds per crab and can be purchased fresh, frozen, or canned.

Fermented black beans—are small black soybeans preserved in salt and generally soaked in water before using. These are also known as Chinese black beans or salty black beans.

Fish sauce—a concentrated salty, brown liquid, typically made from anchovies fermented in brine.

French baguette—a long narrow loaf of French bread that has a crisp crust and chewy interior.

Furikake—a seasoning made from dried seaweed, sesame seeds, and salt that is used to add flavor and color to rice and noodles.

Garbanzo bean—tan-colored legume, also called chickpea.

Garlic—an edible bulb of the lily family containing many cloves. An important part of foods prepared in Hawaii.

Ginger—root of a variety of gingers; the edible ginger is used as a seasoning both in savory dishes (typically with garlic and soy sauce) and in sweets such as cookies, cakes, and candies.

Gobo—Japanese word for the long root vegetable named burdock. Gobo is typically 1/2 to 1-inch in diameter and 12 to 24-inches long.

Goma—See SESAME SEEDS.

Gummy fish—colored gelatinous candies in the form of fish.

Haupia—Hawaiian name given to coconut pudding, but now often used for many coconut-flavored desserts.

Hawaiian chili pepper—a very small (1/2 to 1 inch long) and extremely hot pepper; it ranks about 9 out of 10 on the hotness scale.

Hawaiian chili pepper water—water infused with Hawaiian chili peppers.

Hawaiian escargot—also known as the apple snail. This environmental pest to Hawaiian crops is presently being produced by aquaculture farming.

Hawaiian salt—white coarse sea salt; also see 'ALAEA SALT.

Hawaiian sweet bread—a light weight sweet bread similar to Portuguese sweet bread.

Hibachi—a small grill ("fire bowl" in Japanese). Hibachi cooking is popular in Hawaii.

Hoisin sauce—a thick reddish-brown fermented sweet soy bean sauce that is seasoned with garlic and chili peppers.

'Inamona—Hawaiian word for a relish (in paste or chopped form) made from roasted kukui nuts and usually salt.

Jicama—a large root vegetable with a thin brown skin and a crunchy sweet white flesh. Can be eaten raw or cooked. Also known as the Mexican potato or Chinese yam.

Julienne—to cut a food into thin strips similar to matchsticks.

Kabocha squash—a grayish-green thick-skinned winter squash. It has an orange flesh that is very tender, smooth, and slightly sweet.

Kahlua—coffee-flavored liqueur.

Kahuku shrimp—see PRAWNS.

Kai choy—see MUSTARD CABBAGE.

Kajiki—Japanese name for Pacific blue marlin.

Kali kali—commonly used today to mean 'opakapaka, however in prior times, kale-kale was used to refer to the most mature stage of the 'opakapaka.

Kamaboko—Japanese red or white fish cakes made of pureed white fish mixed with potato starch and salt; then steamed.

Kona coffee—rich coffee made from beans grown in the Kona district on the Big Island of Hawai'i.

Kona crab—is a long-backed crab with a carapace about 9-inches and has large pinchers. It is considered a "red frog crab" and has the Hawaiian name of papa' kua loa.

Kona lobster—see LOBSTER

Kombu—sun-dried sheets of kelp that are used to flavor a variety of cooked foods and sushi. The natural white powder on the dried seaweed contains much of the flavor and should not be rinsed. Also called kelp.

Konnyaku—a gelatinous cake made from the starch of a tuber called devil's tongue. A popular food in Japan, it has little flavor but readily absorbs other flavors.

Kosher salt—a course-grained salt commonly used in Jewish food preparation.

Kukui nuts—the Hawaiian name for the nuts of the candlenut tree; a main component of 'INAMONA.

Lemon grass—a key ingredient in Thai cooking that adds a lemon flavor and fragrance to soups and other dishes. Since the grass is very fibrous, it is not consumed unless ground into a fine powder. It is sometimes substituted for kaffir lime leaves.

Li hing mui powder—a sweet, sour, and salty seasoning traditionally used for Chinese preserved plums; now commonly available as a separate seasoning mix.

Lilikoi—see passion fruit.

Limu—Hawaiian word for all types of plants living in the water or damp places. The use of the word limu today generally applies to only edible seaweeds.

Limu kohu—a highly preferred edible red seaweed that may range in color from tan through shades of pink to dark red (Asparagopsis taxiformis).

Linguine—long, narrow, flat noodles similar to spaghetti, only flat rather than round.

Lobster—a marine crustacean available in various varieties. The Maine lobster has large front claws, whereas the spiny lobster tends to be small and without the large front claws of other varieties of lobster. The Kona lobster is a Spiny variety.

Long rice—translucent thread-like noodles made from mung bean flour. Typically they are soaked in water before cooking.

Lop Cheong or lop chong—this highly seasoned Chinese pork sausage has the dried texture similar to pepperoni and contains a lot of fat.

Lu'au leaf—young taro leaves that must be cooked thoroughly 50-60 minutes before eating.

Lup chong—See LOP CHEONG.

Lychee (lichee)—a small (1 to 2-inches diameter) Chinese fruit with a bright red rough outer shell and a translucent, juicy, sweet, and delicately flavored flesh surrounding a single inner seed. It is typically eaten fresh or canned; when the fruit is dried in the shell, it may be referred to as a lychee nut, but only the dried fruit portion is edible.

Macadamia nuts—a rich flavorful nut that is a major crop in Hawai'i; often called "Mac Nuts".

Mahimahi—also called dolphinfish, but not related to the marine mammal; a mild-flavored firm-fleshed fish.

Mango—a sweet flavorful and aromatic fruit when ripe. Varieties range from greenish-yellow to red in color when ripe with yellow to bright orange flesh. They range 1/4 to 2 pounds and may be smooth or fibrous in texture. Hayden mangoes have a slightly-fibrous pulp.

Maui onions—large white onion noted for its sweet flavor, grown in Kula, the up-country region of Maui. Substitute with other sweet onions, such as Vidalia or Ewa onions.

Mirepoix—a combination of chopped carrots, celery, onions, and herbs sautéed in butter.

Mirin—Japanese sweet rice wine used to add sweetness and flavor to many Japanese dishes. If mirin is unavailable, use 1 tablespoon cream sherry or 1 teaspoon sugar for each tablespoon mirin.

Miso—Japanese word for fermented soybean paste; miso is often used as the base for a broth. There are several varieties that range in color from white to dark brown, with the darker miso more strongly flavored.

Mullet—a silver-grey to silver-blue fish usually 12 to 24 inches in length. This mild-flavored white flesh fish is also known as 'ama 'ama in Hawaiian.

Mussels—a shellfish imported to Hawai'i from New Zealand; sold in local supermarkets frozen, previously frozen, or canned.

Mustard cabbage—a Chinese cabbage known for its pungency and slight bitterness; also known as kai choy and gai choy.

Napa cabbage—also known as celery cabbage, Chinese cabbage, or won bok. Pale green at the top to white at the stem with crinkly leaves.

Nasturtium flowers—generally an orange, yellow, or scarlet-colored edible flowers with a peppery flavor.

Nori—Japanese word for a deep purple or greenish-black seaweed generally sold dried in tissue-thin 8-inch square sheets; frequently used in Japanese cooking, often for wrapping sushi.

Ogo—see LIMU MANUEA.

Onaga—Japanese name for ruby or red snapper.

Ono—a type of fish also called wahoo; a member of the mackerel family, often used for sashimi. Grouper, snapper, or sea bass can be substituted.

Opah—French word for moonfish, a large fish with a rich, full-flavored pinkish flesh. Substitute with swordfish or tuna.

'Opakapaka—Hawaiian name for the pink or crimson snapper.

Oyster mushrooms—a fan-shaped mushroom that varies in color from light gray to dark brownish-gray and has a full flavor.

Oyster sauce—a concentrated dark-brown sauce made from oysters, salt, and soy sauce. Used in many Asian dishes to impart a full, rich flavor. Also available in vegetarian forms.

Panko—Japanese-style bread crumbs, coarser than regular bread crumbs. Substitute with regular unseasoned bread crumbs.

Papaya—in Hawaii this sweet, yellow, pear-shaped fruit is about 6 to 10 inches long. A common size would yield about 1-1/2 to 2 cups flesh.

Passion fruit—a common variety of this fruit in Hawaii has a yellow, shiny outer shell filled inside with seeds surrounded with a juicy pulp. The juice is tangy and unique in flavor. It is also called lilikoi in Hawaiian.

Pa'akai—Hawaiian word for salt or seaweeds that have been prepared with salt.

Pickled ginger—young ginger root sliced thinly and pickled in sweet vinegar. Used as a common Japanese condiment and garnish, typically pink or red in color.

Pine nuts—a high fat nut from several varieties of pine tree; a common ingredient in Italian pesto.

Pineapple—a large (2-5 pounds) pine cone-shaped tropical fruit. Sweet and tangy, it is available primarily in fresh and canned forms.

Pipi kaula—salted and spiced dried beef; literal Hawaiian translation: rope beef.

Poha—Hawaiian word for the cape gooseberry; also known as golden berry, ground cherry, or husk tomato, The yellow, marble-sized fruit hangs on the plant inside a lantern-shaped paper-like "wrapper" (calyx), giving each fruit its own wrapper. It is eaten raw or in jams and pies.

Pohole fern—fiddlehead fern; eaten as the young tightly coiled frond.

Poi—Hawaiian word for cooked taro that is pounded to a paste with the addition of water until it reaches consistency that can be consumed by scooping with one, two, or three fingers.

Poke—Hawaiian word meaning to slice or to cut into small bite-sized pieces; refers to a traditional Hawaiian dish of sliced raw seafood, fresh seaweed, Hawaiian salt, and Hawaiian red chili peppers.

Portuguese sausage—pork sausage with spicing that ranges from mild to hot. Italian sausage can be substituted if necessary

Prawns—although prawns are not the same species of crustacean as shrimp, the term prawn is loosely used to describe any large shrimp, especially those less than 15 per pound.

Preserved black beans—see FERMENTED BLACK BEANS.

Puna goat cheese—rich, creamy cheese made from the milk of goats raised in eastern Big Island region of Puna.

Pupu—the Hawaiian word for appetizer.

Red chili pepper—generic term for many types of chili peppers, generally 1 to 3-inches in length and adding "heat" to the flavor of the dish.

Rice paper wrappers—thin sheets made from rice flour, water, and salt that are used to wrap around meat, fish, or other mixtures for Vietnamese spring rolls.

Rice wine—typically made from steamed glutinous rice, this type of wine is found as various types in Japan such as sake and mirin and in China as chia fan, and yen hung.

Rotini pasta—spiral shaped paste.

Saffron—a bright yellow-orange spice which is considered the world's most expensive spice, but is required in tiny amounts.

Sake—See rice wine.

Sea salt—a salt resulting from the evaporation of sea water and is generally sold in its coarse form.

Sea scallops—see SCALLOPS.

Sesame Oil—oil pressed from the sesame seed is available in two forms. Pressing the raw seed produces an oil which is light in color and flavor and can be used for a wide variety of purposes. When the oil is pressed from the toasted sesame seed, it is dark in color with a much stronger flavor.

Sesame seeds—the seeds of an edible of the Pedaliaceae family which have a distinctive nutty flavor. They come in black and white forms and are fresh or toasted. They are also known as goma in Japan.

Shallot—this member of the onion family forms a bulb more like a garlic bulb and has a more subtle flavor than green onions.

Shiitake mushrooms—Japanese name for a black-to buff-colored mushroom used both fresh and dried. The texture is meaty and the flavor is full. Dried shiitake need to be soaked until soft (20 to 30 minutes). Also called black Chinese mushrooms and forest mushrooms.

Shoyu—see SOY SAUCE

Snow peas—young, edible-podded sugar peas consumed when the pods are thin and the seeds are still tiny.

Somen—Japanese name for a fine light-colored wheat noodle.

Squid—A boneless cephalopod with a white-fleshed body and ten tentacles. It is a bland-flavored meat enjoyed for its firm texture. Also called calamari.

Straw mushrooms—musty flavored, straw-colored mushroom most commonly found in canned form.

Sushi—Japanese word for vinegar flavored rice which surrounds vegetables, spam, or fish. This is sometimes wrapped in a sheet of nori.

Sweet bread—a sweet egg bread, also known as Hawaiian sweet bread or Portuguese sweet bread.

Tamarind—a sweet-tart fruit from pods of the tamarind tree. Sold in pods, powder, and pulp.

Taro—Tahitian word for a starchy root tuber which can be baked or boiled like potatoes or pounded into a paste called poi. The large green taro leaf can be eaten, but must be cooked thoroughly to remove oxalic acid crystals which causes a prickly sensation in the throat. Cooked spinach can be substituted for cooked taro leaf.

Tasso ham—a Cajun spiced smoked ham often found in specialty food shops and used in small finely chopped amounts for flavoring.

Tempura—Japanese word referring to deep-fried foods with a crispy batter coating.

Teriyaki—Japanese word for a marinade or sauce for meat or fish; generally consisting of soy sauce, sugar, ginger, and garlic.

Ti leaf—long slender leaf most easily recognizable from their hula skirt image and used to wrap a variety of foods for cooking. The leaves are not consumed.

Tofu—Japanese name for a bland-flavored soy bean curd that can be custard-like in texture (soft tofu) or quite firm. The firm or extra firm forms are generally used in stir-frying or deep-frying.

Tombo—Japanese word for albacore tuna.

Wasabi—also called Japanese horseradish; comes in both powder and paste forms and is frequently dyed bright green.

Water chestnuts—Crispy white edible tubers of a water plant that have a brownish-black skin resembling a regular chestnut. Available fresh or canned, whole or sliced. Fresh water chestnuts must be peeled before they can be used.

Watercress—a member of the mustard family with crisp dark green leaves that have a slightly bitter and peppery taste.

Wok—a round- or flat-bottomed Chinese cooking pan used for stir-frying or deep-frying foods.

Won bok—A type of Chinese cabbage sometimes referred to as celery cabbage. It is pale green in color with a broad white stem, somewhat similar to romaine lettuce in shape, with a delicate mild flavor.

Won ton wrappers—Very thin sheets of wheat flour and egg dough typically used to make dumplings of different types. Wrappers come in 3-1/2-inch squares and 7-inch squares. The dough can be cut into strips and fried for

See You Next Time   *Index*

Biographies | *"Who Dat?"*

JOANNIE DOBBS • Joannie Dobbs raduated in dietetics from Michigan State University, she holds a Ph.D. in nutrition from the University of California at Davis. She is a Certified Nutrition Specialist (C.N.S.) who has worked in food and nutrition for more than 25 years. As sole proprietor of Exploring New Concepts, Dobbs is a consultant to restaurant chefs and food companies, and does nutrient analyses for various publications. She teaches at the University of Hawai'i Hilo and O'ahu campus. She is co-author of the cookbook, *Bone Appetit,* developed for the Hawai'i Osteoporosis Foundation. She is also a member of the American Culinary Federation's Chef de Cuisine Organization, Hawai'i Chapter. For fun, Joannie creates computer graphics and textile art. Her past also includes five years of study as a Vulture Biologist in South Africa.

ALAN TITCHENAL • "Assistant extraordinaire" to Joannie is her husband, Alan Titchenal. An instructor of food science and human nutrition at the University of Hawai'i, he is an avid surfer even after surviving a shark attack in the Marshall Islands. He received his Bachelor of Arts Degree in ceramics from the University of Hawai'i and his PH.D. from the University of California at Davis. A marathon runner and sports nutritionist, he serves as Chief Score Keeper for the annual Hawai'i International Chili Cookoff.

LYNN COOK • All-day fishing parties at Sand Island, with folks from her Papakolea, O'ahu neighborhood, and thirty-plus years of emersion in the arts and culture of Hawai'i and the Pacific Rim are gifts Lynn Kawaileleowa'ahila Cook strives to share with others. She studied the arts of the First Peoples from childhood through her years working as a feature and food writer on daily papers in the Pacific Northwest. As a travel writer in Hawai'i and the Pacific she covers cultural tourism, festivals, the arts, food, music, romance, and dance for a variety of national magazines. She works with cultural and education organizations, creating programs such as the Kahili Award winning Hawaiian Heritage Cruise series for American Hawaii Cruises, celebrating Aloha Festivals. She studied printmaking in lithography, etching, serigraph and textile design at the University of Washington and the University of Hawai'i. Her prints, exhibited in galleries, gift shops, and Native Books & Beautiful Things, reflect the influence of the "gang she hangs out with — a crowd of thousand-year-old petroglyphs" across the State, from Kaua'i to Hawai'i's Big Island. For total relaxation she dances with Halau Mohala 'Ilima.